THE DEVELOPMENT OF LIBRARY COLLECTIONS OF SOUND RECORDINGS

BOOKS IN LIBRARY AND INFORMATION SCIENCE

A Series of Monographs and Textbooks

EDITOR

ALLEN KENT

Director, Office of Communications Programs
University of Pittsburgh
Pittsburgh, Pennsylvania

Additional volumes in preparation

THE DEVELOPMENT OF LIBRARY COLLECTIONS OF SOUND RECORDINGS

———

Frank W. Hoffmann

LIBRARY SCIENCE DEPARTMENT
SAM HOUSTON STATE UNIVERSITY
HUNTSVILLE, TEXAS

MARCEL DEKKER, INC. New York • Basel

Library of Congress Cataloging in Publication Data

Hoffmann, Frank W   [date]
    The development of library collections of sound
recordings.

    (Books in library and information science; v. 28)
    Bibliography: p.
    Includes indexes.
    1.   Sound recordings--Collectors and collecting.
2.   Sound recording libraries.   I.   Title.   II.   Series.
ML111.5.H57   025.2   79-23064
ISBN 0-8247-6858-2

MARCEL DEKKER, INC.

270 Madison Avenue, New York, New York 10016

Current printing (last digit):
10 9 8 7 6 5 4 3 2 1

PRINTED IN THE UNITED STATES OF AMERICA

To L.A.B.

Some feelings outlast the printed word

Each week several hundred records and pre-recorded tapes are
released by American companies alone within the recorded sound
industry. The majority of them either never see the light of
day or are forgotten shortly after they gain the collective ear
of the nation. A solid minority of these relaeses, however,
merit inclusion in library collections because of either
aesthetic, sociological, or mass appeal considerations. The
primary dilemmas faced by librarians are as follows:

1. Learning how to approach the area of sound recordings
   with complete objectivity and some degree of personal
   understanding, thereby enabling librarians to take an
   active part in determining those works to be rescued
   from imminent oblivion.

2. Ascertaining the most efficient means of determining
   those recordings which deserve to be included in library collections.

3. Finding a means of monitoring the needs and interests
   of the clientele which a given library is supposed to
   be serving.

In this book, I have attempted to provide a blueprint of
the selection, acquisition, and arrangement of phonorecords and
tapes in all types of libraries. It is my belief that the work
fills several gaps within the literature of this area:

1. The majority of general texts on materials selection
   have devoted a comparatively small amount of space to
   the discussion of nonprint items.

2. Books dealing with the development of record collections have tended to emphasize classical music recordings. Rock music, which accounts for over one-half
   of the sales of all recordings, has generally been
   ignored in the discussion of library disc and tape
   collections.

3. While texts have been written which deal with the
   development of record collections, little has been
   said about the inclusion of pre-recorded tapes in
   library collections.

4. There exists virtually no information in the library
   literature concerning the evaluation of the reviewing
   media for sound recordings.

This work aims at being a textbook in the broadest sense
of that term. I have sought to provide an introductory source-
book for library school students concerned with materials
selection (of which sound recordings have become an increasingly
important part) as well as an everyday, practical guide for
professionals already active in the field in a variety of library settings.

CONTENTS

THE DEVELOPMENT OF LIBRARY COLLECTIONS OF SOUND RECORDINGS

Libraries are presently attempting to resolve the dilemma of
being unable, in the face of declining support or apathy on the
part of their respective clientele, to justify the continually
rising budgetary allotments required merely to maintain existing levels of efficiency. The planning and implementation of
exotic new programs, seen by some as the universal panacea for
this problem, would seem to run contrary to the dictates of
sound fiscal management as well as to fail to connect with the
central needs and interests of the general public. It would
appear that an emphasis upon doing well what librarians have
traditionally done represents a logical starting point in the
upgrading of library services. By "traditional" functions,
the author is implying the acquisition, circulation, and inter-
pretative utilization of graphic materials. The development
of record and tape collections in libraries represents an important facet of the library's role as an agency responsible
for the selection, preservation, and interpretation of graphic
records. Libraries, however, have often fallen short of their
potential in the recorded sound collections sector.

HISTORY OF SOUND RECORDINGS IN LIBRARIES

The first documented record collection within the public library sector was begun in St. Paul, Minnesota as the result of
a resident's gift of his small collection of records in 1913
or 1914.[1] This collection was limited to use only by schools
and clubs. From these inauspicious beginnings some thirty-
seven years after the invention of the phonograph player,
growth progressed at a slow and erratic pace. By 1939, 17
towns in the United States with populations of 75,00 or more
possessed record collections.[2] Literature on the subject was
also slow to appear; it was not until 1936 that a noticeably
large selection of articles on record collections could be
found in the library literature.[3] These contributions revealed
a great degree of variation within librarianship with respect
to standards of selection as well as methods of cataloging,
classification, and loan procedure. By the fifties, books had
begun to appear which provided a detailed analysis of record
selection principles (e.g. Bryant's *Music Librarianship*); these
publications lagged more than a decade behind primers outside
the library field by experts such as Howard Taubman, Bernard
Haggin, and David Hall.

With a few notable exceptions, libraries have been noto-
riously slow in providing adequate record and tape resources to
users over the past twenty-five years. A representative policy
during this period has been that outlined in the American Library Association's *Costs of Public Library Service in 1959*:

> For a community of 50,000 a minimum of 2.9 per cent
> of the book budget should be spent on records. The
> proportion is less as the size of the community in-
> creases...

> Cost figures soon become obsolete, but those given
> for a minimum standard in 1959 have not yet been
> reached by many libraries. For a community of
> 50,000 an annual record budget of $1050 was recom-
> mended for 300 recordings...[4]

The proportion devoted here to recordings is alarmingly low; yet many public libraries have yet to match these figures.

The present status of record and tape collections in other types of libraries reveals a similar lack of planning and consistency in policy making. The recorded disc has been a viable commercial entity since the turn of the century; however, as indicated by the above American Library Association policy statement, libraries by and large continue to treat it as a poor cousin of the printed page. Collections of sound recordings frequently lack both the depth and balance characteristic of book and periodical holdings.

Various scholars and practitioners within the field of librarianship have provided enlightened ideas relating to library record collection development. The concerted efforts of these individuals, however, have not been sufficient to result in the promulgation of a meaningful plan of action with respect to record selection procedures. Gordon Stevenson feels that this problem is largely a result of the fact that librarianship, since becoming involved with records and tapes, has had little contact with or understanding of the recorded sound industry.[5] A major reason for this situation, according to Stevenson, lies in the absence of communications channels of mutual interest between the library field and the record and tape companies.[6] He backs up his argument by contrasting this relationship with that existing between librarianship and the book trade:

> book publishing and its technical aspects of production, aesthetic aspects of print, and the social and psychological implications of books and reading have all been integrated into the profession. In no single case can librarianship be said to have even begun to integrate similar knowledge of recorded sound into this prfession.[7]

Don Roberts, in 1970, saw the weakness of libraries within the area of record collection development as being part of an even greater problem; the failure of the profession to display much sensitivity to the acquisition of popular culture materials:

> We have a negative commitment to the popular culture of our society, even though this culture (especially in the music industry) is of the highest it has been for many, many generations. The shocking, repetitious print equivalent stuff pouring out of the publishing houses is reviewed, purchased, and processed toward oblivion on the shelves regardless, while the Number One recorded literature is not even considered! And so we continue to run the vestiges of a defunct Western humanism and post-Renaissance classicism (typified in a way by the Caldecott/ Newbery awards and our book selection mystiques) on the hapless, cynical library dropout taxpayers and their children.[8]

From January to June of 1976, the author surveyed 1003 community members and 57 public librarians (representing 35 libraries), randomly selected from the population of Allegheny County, Pennsylvania.[9] The objectives of the study were as follows:

1. To provide a barometer of the current attitudes held by community members and librarians with respect to public library record collections

2. To identify those demographic subgroups whose buying habits and recommendations for library record holdings reveal them to be at odds with the present selection policies of the public library

3. To compare the relative influence of the public library with that of commercial agencies in determining the listening tastes and buying patterns of the public

4. To encourage the library profession to employ a greater degree of objectivity in assessing its performance, to date, in the area of record collection development

The study yielded the following insights:

1. Types of music recordings purchased most frequently
    by respondents:

    Community

    rock, 36%; soul and blues, 20%; pop, 15%; country,
    10%; jazz, 9%; classical, 7%; folk, 2%

    Librarians

    classical. 30%; pop, 28%; rock, 19%; soul, jazz,
    folk, 5%; country, 0%

2. Proportions of classical music to popular music in
    record collections of participating public libraries:
    100% classical, 0 libraries; 75% classical/25% pop,
    8 libraries; 50% of each, 13 libraries; 75% pop/25%
    classical, 10 libraries; 100% pop, 1 library. (Three
    libraries were not applicable because they did not
    possess any records.)

3. Annual record budget of the public libraries included
    in the study: more than $1000, 6 libraries; $501-
    1000, 3 libraries; $251-500, 10 libraries; $1-250, 8
    libraries; none (gifts only), 8 libraries

4. Record collection total for public libraries partici-
    pating in the study: 10,000 or more, 1 library; 5001-
    10,000, no libraries; 1501-5000, 7 libraries; 500-
    1500, 11 libraries; under 500, 13 libraries; none, 3
    libraries

In summary, library service within the realm of sound recordings has left a lot to be desired up to the present. The
successful implementation of a blueprint which would realize
the democratic philosophy of service outlined in the Library
Bill of Rights necessitates at least two traits on the part of
librarians:

1. A firm commitment by the profession to actively
    promote library use

2. Sufficient enlightenment and conviction on the part
    of librarians to overcome their own personal preju-
    dices in order to be completely objective in carrying
    out their professional responsibilities

A SURVEY OF STANDARDS

The various standards concerned with the inclusion of sound
recordings in library collections indicate that the profession's sacred cows die hard. The preeminence accorded the
print format has been eroded little by the increasing importance of audiovisual media within our society.

The sound recordings industry presently accounts for retail sales of almost $3 billion annually.[10] A figure not far
short of the total receipts per year grossed by the book
trade.[11] In contrast to this state of affairs, the *Minimum
Standards for Public Library Systems, 1966* reveals a wide
discrepancy between book and recorded sound collection recommendations. For a library system serving a population ranging
from 150,000 to 1,000,000 it has been recommended that public
library headquarters contain at least 100,000 adult nonfiction
titles as the foundation of the collection, while the total
system holdings provide at least 2 to 4 volumes per capita.[12]
In contrast to these figures, the Public Library Association
had the following to say with respect to sound recordings:

> The basic collection of recordings for the system
> should consist of one disc or reel of tape for each
> 50 people in the service area, but no collection
> should contain less than 5000 discs and reels.
> Selected recordings should be duplicated to meet
> needs and to supply rotating collections for the
> system, if such are desired.[13]

The Association of College and Research Libraries' *Standards for College Libraries* makes recommendations which are
considerably more vague than those outlined above. Breakdowns
for audiovisual media (as opposed to print materials) are not
present in this source. The language is couched in general-
ities such as:

The college librarian shall have the responsibility
for preparing, defending, and administering the
library budget in accord with agreed-upon objectives.[14]

and:

The library shall maintain a systematic and continuous
program for evaluating its performance and for identifying needed improvements.[15]

The American Association of School Librarians has provided the following recommendations in *Media Programs: District
and School*:

It is recommended that a school with 500 or fewer
students have a minimum collection of 20,000 items
or 40 per student. An item is defined as a book
(casebound or paperback), film, videotape, filmstrip,
transparency, slide, periodical subscription, kit, any
other form of material, or associated equipment. It
is possible that the collection in larger schools may
provide the needed range in content, levels, forms
of expression, and formats at a ratio of less than
40 items per student.[16]

This total collection has been itemized to include 8000 to
12,000 book volumes (16 to 24 per user) with access to 60,000
titles via loans from other sources.[17] Audio recordings
(i.e. tapes, cassettes, discs, and audio cards) have been
recommended in quantities of 1500 to 2000 (3 to 4 per user)
with access to 5000 recordings by means of outside sources.[18]

The low figures recommended for sound recordings in comparison with book statistics would appear unjustified for the
following reasons:

1. The innate appeal of this medium, particularly among
    youth, the group which comprises the majority of
    public, school, and college library audiences, re-
    spectively

2. The documented importance of sound recording as an
    educational tool

3. The optimum availability of records and tapes, often
    at exceptionally reasonable prices, when compared to
    books possessed of serious educational value

A TENTATIVE LOOK TO THE FUTURE

In the face of continually rising public consumption of sound
recordings, as well as increased attention to the phenomenon
by the mass media, it would appear safe to predict that librarians in all types of libraries will provide the impetus
necessary for the development of future collections which contain higher proportions of tapes and records than is characteristic of the present. The chief question here is whether
or not the profession will move quickly enough to satisfy the
interests and needs of its audience, or come to find that they
have moved on to other agencies which have supplied their
demands more efficiently. This unfortunate situation has
already been partially set in motion. Retailers, radio and
television stations, community centers, and enthusiastic collectors have all beaten libraries at the starting gate. Enlightened decision making in the future, however, would enable
the library to make a stronger showing as its competitors continue to gather up momentum. The services which libraries
could provide in conjunction with strong collections of sound
recordings are multifold. A sampling of these include (a) the
resources behind a radio station (some libraries actually run
their own broadcasting facilities); (b) programming for group
activities; (c) the backdrop for theatrical, civic, etc.,
presentations; (d) a valuable information reservoir for the
answering of reference questions (i.e. the use of liner notes
and album song selections); and (e) the production of tapes
for researchers and other interested individuals. While it is
important that an awareness of the need for stronger collections be reflected in the various standards, a far more

important development would be for this realization to catch hold on a grass-roots level.

NOTES

1. Eric Thomas Bryant, *Music Librarianship; A Practical Guide*, Clarke, London, 1963, p. 185.

2. *Ibid.*

3. *Ibid.*

4. Public Library Association, American Library Association, *Costs of Public Library Service in 1959, A Supplement to Public Library Service: A Guide to Evaluation, with Minimum Standards*, American Library Association, Chicago, 1959, p. 9.

5. Gordon Stevenson, "Sound Recordings," *Advances in Librarianship*, 5, Academic, New York, 1975, p. 286.

6. *Ibid.*

7. *Ibid.*

8. Don Roberts, "Listen, Miss, Mrs., Mr. Librarian," *School Library Journal*, November, 1970, p. 30.

9. Frank W. Hoffmann, *A Methodological Study of Librarian and Community Attitudes Concerning Public Library Phonorecord Collections in Allegheny County*, Ph.D Thesis, University of Pittsburgh, 1977.

10. "Rock Music Business," *Editorial Research Reports*, June 10, 1977, p. 450.

11. *The Bowker Annual of Library & Book Trade Information, 1977*, 22d ed., edited and compiled by Nada Glick and Sarah Prakken, Bowker, New York, 1977, p. 319.

12. *Minimum Standards for Public Library Systems, 1966*, prepared by the Standards Committee and Subcommittees of the Public Library Association, American Library Association, Chicago, 1967, p. 42.

13. *Ibid*, p. 45.

14. *Standards for College Libraries*, Association of College and Research Libraries, Chicago, 1975, Revision of the 1959 standards, p. 23.

15. *Ibid*, p. 20.

16. *Media Programs: District and School*, prepared by the American Association of School Librarians, American Library Association, and the Association for Educational Communications and Technology, Chicago and Washington, D.C., 1975, p. 69.

17. *Ibid*, p. 70.

18. *Ibid*, p. 79.

Chapter 1

GENERAL PRINCIPLES OF SELECTION

INTRODUCTION

While there exists a paucity of literature concerned with the
general principles of selection as they specifically relate
to sound recordings, many articles and books have been written
outlining these principles in the area of book selection.
Perhaps the major reason for this shortage in the library literature can be attributed to the fact that these principles
usually apply to recordings as well as print materials. The
most important of these general principles are as follows:

1. It is imperative that the library know the character
    of the clientele which it serves.

2. No subgroup within this clientele (i.e., persons
    distinguished by nationality, creed, or belief system)
    should be excluded from consideration in the selection
    process.

3. The following variables ought to be integrated into
    selection procedures:
    a. Demand
    b. High standards of quality
    c. Purpose
    d. Need

(The ordering of priorities with respect to this listing of factors depends upon the service philosophy of
the particular library in question.)

4. Each library collection should be developed in accordance with a preconceived set of objectives.

5. Despite the need to recognize the nuances of every
   library's clientele, the core of the collection should
   be devoted to holdings capable of a widespread application.

6. Whatever materials fit into the various service phi-
   losophies of the library (i.e., recreational, educational, or archival) ought to be represented in the
   collection to some degree.

METHODS OF OBTAINING NONUSERS' VIEWS

A wide variety of means exist by which a library can acquire
a knowledge of the patrons utilizing its materials and resources. An obvious method consists of communicating with
users of the library at times when they come within that setting. This technique has the disadvantage of not including
the opinions of those individuals who do not utilize the library. Nonusers' views can be obtained by any of the following
approaches:

1. Random distribution of questionnaires via the mail,
   community pick-up points, or door-to-door distribution

2. Oral interviewing on a random basis of selection at
   certain community outposts

3. Interviewing by telephone of randomly chosen individuals

4. Monitoring of record and tape sales at important retail outlets serving the same clientele

5. Monitoring of concert receipts and radio song requests
   of this clientele

It should be noted that each of these approaches carries built-
in disadvantages. For example, the use of telephones discrim-

inates against that sector of the population that does not own them.

Perhaps the most accurate tool in obtaining nonusers' views (as well as those of users) is that of the written questionnaire. A good written questionnaire should include as many as possible of the following items:

Amount of recordings (33-rpm, 45 rpm, and tapes) purchased annually

Type of music purchased most frequently

Agencies which have most influenced buying habits

Agencies which have most influenced musical tastes

Types of sound recordings which should be carried in larger amounts

Proportions of classical music to popular music which would be best for a given library collection

Whether a given library allows the recommendation of desired sound recordings

Whether or not the respondent has ever possessed a library card or checked out recordings

Relevant demographic information (e.g. marital status, income, level of educational attainment, and age)

The collecting of such demographic information will enable the library to better anticipate the needs and interests of various subgroups within the overall clientele. The greatest problem revolves around the reticence which some respondents might express over providing data relating to their personal lives. It is of paramount importance that these individuals be enlightened as to the benefits to be derived from the disclosure of demographic data.

Type of library is probably the key consideration in the ordering of priorities in the selection process. Public libraries are likely to place the greatest emphasis upon the demand variable, whereas college and research libraries tend to stress the purpose factor. The need variable applies to

special situations in which gaps in the collection are revealed
that require immediate rectification, even to the extent that
quality is not necessarily to be of the highest level with respect to the recordings acquired in order to overcome such
failings. High standard of quality should always represent an
important variable; indeed, its presence ideally ought to be
felt no matter what other variable may be receiving top-
priority consideration. The need variable can make itself
known either by the voiced opinions of users or the more indi-
rect route characterized by ascertaining nonusers' opinions in
the form of specific additions to the holdings of sound recordings, it is imperative that this sector be made aware of these
inclusions by means of the proper public relations channels.

THE DEVELOPMENT OF A SELECTION POLICY

The need for a library collection to be developed according to
a premeditated set of goals cannot be emphasized enough. The
best means of assuring the presence of this process is through
the formulation of a well-outlined selection policy. For those
collections which have existed for some time previous to the
writing up of such a policy, special attention will probably be
necessary in the area of immediate objectives as well as long-
term goals so as to ensure the most efficient possible development. A policy statement concerned with sound recordings s
should take into account the following concepts:

1. A means of offsetting the presence of latent bias on
    the part of various staff members
2. A means of protecting the library against attacks from
    its clientele with respect to censorship activities
3. A means of delineating the breakdown of the collection
    as to genre, speed, format, etc.
4. A means of ascertaining the level of quality required
    of all acquisitions to the collection

5. A means of outlining the needs and future projections of the collection

Terminology of a vague, flowery, or overly idealistic nature should be avoided in the formulation of a selection policy. The order of the day is for clear-cut and realistic goals.

DIFFERENCES IN APPROACH DICTATED BY TYPE OF LIBRARY

It is necessary to recognize certain norms in the development of collections of sound recordings, at least with regard to each type of library. These norms include the following for public libraries:

1. The recreational factor will figure prominantly in the selection process.

2. Accordingly, although this genre has application to the educative function as well, popular music should comprise the bulk of the collection.

3. Offerings which tend to appeal to minorities ought to be stocked in large quantities only by large libraries. Ideally provisions should exist for these smaller libraries in the form of interlibrary loan channels so as to assure that little-requested recordings can be obtained with a minimum of inconvenience.

The norms for college, university, and research libraries include:

1. The educative function, both in terms of curriculum demands and advanced scholarship, receives the greatest emphasis with respect to collection-building.

2. The educative process used to concern itself almost completely with classical music and spoken-work recordings of dramatic, poetic, or instructional bents; however, popular genres are just as likely to be the objects of serious research at the present time. The structuring of a curriculum has much to do with determining just what recordings can be employed as part of the educative process.

School libraries used to refer students to public libraries for the provision of popular music recordings. The
general failure of public libraries, however, to adequately
provide records and tapes in this area, in addition to increasing demands from their clientele, has caused school libraries
to place greater emphasis upon the inclusion of the popular
genres. As has been the case with academic institutions,
school libraries are likely to include virtually any genre of
sound recordings in attempting to datisfy curricular demands
on the part of students and faculty.

Special libraries are a varied lot which tend to fall into
three distinct classes:

1. Those emulating public libraries in their service
    philosophy and the diversity of their clientele
    (e.g., mental hospital and prison libraries).

2. Specialized research collections (either of a private
    or commercial nature) which closely mirror the
    approach of college and university libraries. They
    focus upon almost any subject imaginable; the variety
    is endless.

3. Museum holdings, often administered by governmental
    or nonprofit agencies, which tend to reflect the
    educational and research interests of college and
    research libraries.

Chapter 2

SELECTION CRITERIA FOR SOUND RECORDINGS

SUBJECTIVITY IN THE SELECTION OF SOUND RECORDINGS

While recognizing the need for a written selection policy dealing with books, many libraries have failed to apply a similar scheme of logic to the audio recordings sector. Rather, the tendency has been to merely append a statement or paragraph concerning recordings to the text of the general materials statement. The most noteworthy result of this situation has been that the personal inclinations of librarians have taken precedence over structured policy making. One frequent manifestation of this reliance upon subjectivity has been the relative absence of popular music recordings in library collections in comparison with retail sales breakdowns. The causes for selecting recordings in small quantities are reflected in the learnings of librarians themselves; these causes include

1. The innate belief that popular music is aesthetically inferior to classical music. The cardinal error here is that of judging the merits of a given popular work in accordance with the criteria characterizing the evaluation of a serious opus. For

instance, it would be futile to assess the intrinsic artistry of Janis Joplin, who many consider to be the finest exponent of white blues of all time, according to the standards expected of an opera singer.

2. The "temporary popularity" bias, i.e., the belief that a popular music recording ceases to attract interest on the part of library clientele after its initial run of popularity. In truth, there exists no foundation for such a belief. Record charts are not an accurate gauge for potential library circulation. The charts, which are usually based upon sales, jukebox action, and radio plays, reflect the popularity of a disc only at its highest point. Many popular recordings, however, retain a comparative degree of popularity far outdistancing that of most serious music compositions long after their disappearance from the charts. The recent revival of ragtime and rural blues, as well as the continued popularity of the album output of rock groups such as the Beatles and the Rolling Stones, reflects this state of affairs. In a library setting, the above recordings might well produce optimum circulation figures.

3. A bias against recreational materials. Some librarians tend to favor items which carry an obvious educational tag. Part of the problem here lies in the failure of the profession to take a broader view of what the educational process entails.

4. A bias against nonprint materials, which continues to plague the profession. While most librarians are committed to the need for representative collections of nonprint items, such media are viewed as something less than top priority. Therefore, nonprint budgetary allotments rarely hold their own against the fiscal demands of print materials, particularly in this era of shrinking library funding.

5. Another means of rationalization against the adequate representation of popular music recordings has been the proneness of these materials to damage and theft. This problem can be attributed to the fact that a large portion of the audience for pop music is comprised of youths, who tend to be less responsible and conscientious than the average adult user. Rather than resigning themselves to this state of affairs, a more constructive approach on the part of librarians to attempt to meet the problem head on at a causal level.

6. The more exoteric pop recordings are often hard to
    obtain. Retailing outlets tend to concentrate on
    the most popular discs, with the more obscure items
    being available only by means of mail order directly
    from the company. This problem is complicated by
    the fact that many of these recordings go rapidly
    out of print.

7. A lack of knowledge of this field on the part of many
    librarians.

EDUCATION OF LIBRARIANS

Many professionals have chosen to default on the issue of
whether or not to include pop music within library collections
rather than undertake the necessary preparation in order to
function in an objective and enlightened manner. The key
word here is education ; there exists a wide variety of means
by which librarians can effectively (and painlessly) learn
about popular recordings, assuming that they are willing to
take the trouble to do so.

First, and foremost, listen closely to popular songs and
compositions. No substitute exists for a first-hand acquain-
tance with the music one is attempting to evaluate.

Second, read about popular music and the people who make
it. Books offer the advantage of often providing a condensed
overview of the genre, whether the treatment be that of a
history, selective discography (with or without annotations),
or anthology of record reviews. Noteworthy examples of each
of these can be found in Appendix 1. Ephemeral publications
such as song broadsides and promo sheets (distributed by
record companies, radio stations, or commercial agencies)
represent another form of education via reading. Probably
the most important subclass within the print heading is that
of the serial. Serials can be divided into a number of
subcategories:

1. Music trade publications (e.g., *Billboard, Variety,*
    Cash Box, Record World), which are aimed primarily
    at commercial retail and broadcast outlets. Gauging
    sales and popularity potential is the primary aim
    of these magazines, rather than assessing the aes-
    thetic qualities of various recordings.

2. Fanzines such as *Circus, Creem,* and *Hit Parader,*
    geared at a predominantly under-twenty-one audience.
    While hese magazines are written on an adolescent
    level (often by young adults themselves), they are
    informative and possess a competant and engaging
    style, which succeeds in imparting some of the flavor
    of the pop scene. They tend to include large review
    sections devoted primarily to rock albums.

3. Journals providing a serious treatment of music (e.g.,
    Stereo Review, High Fidelity, Rolling Stone, Melody
    Maker, Crawdaddy). *Stero Review* and *High Fidelity*
    are equally divided between classical and popular
    music, whereas the others concentrate upon the pop-
    ular idioms. All of them include an assortment of
    feature articles, news notes, and reviews. The
    analysis in each reveals a high degree of insight,
    perhaps the best of all of the mass-produced per-
    iodicals concerned predominantly with music.

4. The more broadly based publications dealing with music
    on an occasional basis or as a minor feature. This
    category includes, on the scholarly front, the
    Journal of Popular Culture and *Sing Out*; and in the
    commercial arena, *Saturday Review, The New Yorker,*
    Time, Newsweek, and *Ebony*.

5. The library literature also includes periodic fea-
    tures concerned with popular music (e.g., *Library*
    Journal, School Library Journal, Previews, Wilson
    Library Bulletin, American Libraries). These articles,
    although sporadic in their occureance, are partic-
    ularly valuable for their direct relationship to the
    profession's greatest problem in the popular music
    area, i.e., how to objectively evaluate and select
    recordings for library collections. *Previews,* the
    nonprint arm of the Bowker complex, is the only li-
    brary journal to include reviews of pop recordings
    on a regular basis. A more comprehensive look at
    periodicals relating to music appears in Chapter 3.

Finally, encourage professional organizations within the field of librarianship (e.g., the American Library Association, as well as its subdivisions such as the Public Library Association, Children's Services Division, and Young Adult Services Division) to pay greater attention to popular music. Some of the ways in which these organizations might assist librarians in the selection of sound recordings would be the compilation of stock lists, the institution of awards for excellence in popular music discs, and the dissemination of infromative guidelines concerned with record collection development.

Other aids in the selection process, for classical as well as popular recordings, include radio and television programming, concerts, organizations and agencies involved with sound recordings, local retail stores, seminars, conventions, and local resource people. The latter group can be utilized either by means of oral communication or the development of a resource file.

EVALUATIVE CRITERIA IN THE SELECTION OF SOUND RECORDINGS

As noted in Chapter 1, the core of an enlightened selection procedure is the presence of a written policy concerned solely with sound recordings. Such a policy is contingent upon the formulation of various evaluative criteria. The major categories of these criteria are:

1. The performance, which includes artistry and/or musicianship, recording quality, and disc/tape quality
2. Reputation of the composer, artisits and/or musicians, record company, etc
3. Complementary print material
4. Packaging of the sound recording
5. Extra features

6. A comparison of the formats available

7. Availability of the recording

8. Potential popularity with its inteded audience

THE PERFORMANCE CRITERION

The performance factor comprises the meat of the evaluative process. In essence, the sound one hears in a finished product is the result of three indepencent variables:

1. The quality of the artist's performance, whether it be a poetry reading, dramatic work, comic routine, or musical offering

2. The quality of the production of the recording

3. The physical quality of the disc/tape medium

To the educated listener, the artistry variable represents the most important aspect in evaluating the overall sound of a given recording. While the other two variables function to enhance the appeal of a recording, they cannot overcome the deficiencies inherent in a poor performance. A superior performance, however, can be greatly undermined by mediocre studio engineering and/or a shoddy disc pressing.

The following considerations go into a complete assessment of the artistry of a sound recording:

1. The technical proficiency displayed by the performers involved

2. The nature of the performance, i.e., whether the recording was produced live, in the studio, or out in the field

3. The message or intent of the composer, artist(s), etc

4. Its value as a social document

The evaluation of these points will ultimately remain a subjective process. However, a modicum of objectivity might be maintained by close adherence to the ground rules characterizing the particular genre assessed in a given situation.

The factors comprising an evaluation of the recording quality of a disc or tape are (a) the mix of the instruments (e.g., muddy, hot, dampened beneath the vocals); (b) the environment in which the recording took place; (c) the type of fidelity employed (i.e., stereophonic, monaural, electronically reprocessed stereo, or quadraphonic); (d) the nature of the channel separation (e.g., the presence or absence of crossover); (e) the appearance of extraneous noise connected with the recording process, such as distortion or sounds not intended to be picked up by the microphones; and (f) special characteristics of note (e.g., the use of electronic feedback, studio echo, editing of the original take or takes, the dubbing in of additional vocal and/or instrumental lines).

An assessment of the physical characteristics of the disc medium includes (a) the amount of pops, ticks, and other surface noise; (b) the degree of warpage; (c) the quality of the vinyl with respect to its potential for wear; (d) the presence of scratches or other marks caused by the production process; (e) whether or not a record has been repackaged; (f) the quality of the pressing (i.e., poorly produced discs may be characterized by distortion, offcenter stamping, jagged or nicked edges, etc.); and (g) the presence of foreign matter embedded in the grooves of a record, such as paper or steel wire from the process of scraping the labels off of discs which are to be recycled.

Following a gradual process of refinement and improvement in the quality of the long-playing album since its initial appearance in 1948, the energy crisis of 1973 signaled the beginning of a decline in the grade of the product turned out.

Since both the acetate base of tapes and the vinyl used in
records are manufactured primarily from oil, the recorded
sound industry has been profoundly affected by the shortage
(theoretical or otherwise) of this vital commodity. As the
sale of units continued to rise steadily, it became necessary
to spread out the amount of polyvinyl used for each disc or
tape. This has been accomplished (a) by the inclusion of more
filler materials in the blend poured into the stamping machine,
and (b) by making the records thinner and tapes shorter (i.e.,
to play at a slower speed); in other words, the use of less
oil-based raw material in the pressing process per unit.
Accordingly, a number of problems have become manifest since
1973. The wafer-thin character of recent discs, combined with
the shrink-wrap plastic used to package American albums, has
resulted in an alarming increase in the rate of disc warpage.
The increased amount of filler has led to a noticeable rise
in the level of surface noise detectable in a record. Increasing reliance upon the recycling of old records also has
resulted in an upsurge in the incidence of production flaws,
while the presence of an inferior grade of vinyl has led to
the appearance of distortion on a greater number of virgin
pressings.

     Prerecorded tapes present their own particular types of
problems. In order to render them a feasible commodity, record
companies have cut down on the amount of tape utilized (by
means of switching from a playback speed of 7 ½ to 3 3/4
inches per second) and have reproduced the recorded output at
very high speeds. The result of the latter practice has been
a large amount of distortion and tape hiss detectable to even
the most inexperienced listener.

THE REPUTATION CRITERION

The reputation variable includes many considerations of a more
subjective nature. With respect to the composer, it is concerned with (a) the quality of the corpus of his output; (b)
the particular style(s) which he employs; and (c) his relevance
in relation to a given event, trend, school of thought, etc.
The reputation of an artist would be concerned with his exper-
tise as a musician, actor, speaker, or comedian, as well as
with the unique talents and/or flaws inherent in his performance. For example, an opera singer's distressing tendency to
slur the syllables of words beyond recognition might be for-
given in the face of an extraordinarily lovely tone in the
upper register. In assessing the reputation of a record
company, one would have to take into consideration (a) the
musical inclinations, stylistically speaking, previously ex-
hibited by the label; (b) the degree of promotion which it
provides; (c) the quality of the artists within its stable;
and (d) the money and effort expended by the company in helping
the artisit realize his intentions. It should be kept in mind
that such points are meant to be utilized as guidelines only,
and that the reputation of a composer, artist, or record company previous to a given instance does not necessarily provide
sufficient evidence to predict the character of a future product. Generally speaking, a librarian should rely only upon
authoritative sources when unable to preview a recording first-
hand.

COMPLEMENTARY PRINT MATERIAL

The nature of complementary print material, while rarely the
primary determining factor in the selection of sound recordings,
may well be the ultimate discriminating consideration if all

other things are equal. Much valuable information concerning
a given recording can be obtained by means of these sources.
These materials include (a) liner notes, (b) libretti, (c)
photo albums, and (d) song lyrics enclosed either on a separate sheet or on the album cover itself. The liner notes
should be judged as to their authenticity, accuracy, objectivity, and the amount of information present. There may well
be exceptions to these criteria; for example, an album cover
which utilizes questionable superlatives in assessing the artistic worth of a certain rock group could be considered worthy of inclusion in a library collection in view of an imaginative or striking type of prose. The fact that a famous per-
sonage has written the notes may also render them of interest.
The aesthetic value of any photographic inclusions (whether
on the cover or within a booklet) may represent an aspect
meriting attention at selection time. The descriptive character of these illustrations might also demand notice. The
artwork on album covers in general has developed spectacularly
over the past fifteen years.

The literary qualitiy and accuracy of representation characteristic of printed song lyrics and libretti should be the
key considerations in their evaluation. The strength of the
translation represents the most vital feature for assessment
when dealing with the libretti of operas and other dramatic
works in foreign languages. Lyric sheets and libretti often
include attractive illustrations which greatly enhance their
overall appeal.

PACKAGING OF SOUND RECORDINGS

The packaging of sound recordings is even less likely than the
nature of auxiliary print material to influence the selection
process. However, this variable can occasionally be an impor-

tant factor in view of the highly competivitive character of
the record industry. This is especially easy to appreciate
when one realizes that the recorded output of a given artist
often competes with itself in the form of reissues. Facets
of record packaging which should be evaluated include (a) the
sturdiness of the jacket construction, (b) the attractiveness
of the cover art, (c) the composition of the inside sleeve,
and (d) the type of jacket employed.

   A wide variety of jacket styles for albums have made their
appearance on the market; a large percentage of them probably
as a result of the personal idiosyncracies or preferences of
certain pop artists. The most frequently employed types are
the unipak, the twin pack, the box, and the regular format.
The regular style is comprised of two cardboard portions pasted
together so as to form a simple sandwich around the disc. The
twin pack is essentially two regular jackets connected by a
creased cardboard spine. The unipak consists of a 12-inch
square piece of cardboard folded over the open side of the
regular album format. The fact that the record is completely
enclosed until the flap is opened up represents an advance in
the care and preservation of records. The unipak, along with
the twin pack, also provides a greater opportunity for artistic
expression due to the additional connecting panels on both the
inside and outside. The box is used primarily for operas,
dramatic works and musical anthologies. Some of the problems
associated with boxes are (a) the frequency with which the
paper used to secure the two halves of the box together is
torn apart, (b) the ease with which these boxes are likely to
warp, and (c) the susceptibility of records inside to warpage
due to the lack of sufficient support in storage. An advantage
of boxes is that they permit the inclusion of as many as several
libretti, catalogs, song lyric booklets, etc.

Except for the previously noted weak binding of boxes,
the leading jacket types are all relatively sturdy in their
construction. Many of the one-shot designs inspired by a
particular artist, however, are somewhat less well put together. An example which comes readily to mind is Jethro Tull's
Stand Up (Reprise), which features an insert constructed in
such a way as to pop up each time the twin pack is opened.
Another problem with some of these unusual jackets is that
they are streamlined in such a way as to leave a large portion
of the disc unprotected from surface scratches and the impact
of rough handling.

EXTRA FEATURES

A number of features exist which are not the norm with respect
to recordings. These characteristics are usually not intrin-
sically related to the aesthetic facets of a disc. They include (a) the design of the label on the record, (b) the color
of the vinyl, and (c) various gimmicks such as a "three-sided"
record (i.e., Johnny Winter's *Second Winter*, which consists
of a double record set with one side left blank) and the presence of special album covers (e.g., the red felt coating of
the Bee Gees' *Odessa*).

Record discs made the use of colored vinyl rather than
the customary black have always been treated by enthusiasts
as collectors' items. They first appeared in comparatively
large numbers during the late fifties on 45-rpm doo-wop discs
(i.e., rhythm and blues vocal groups). These discs usually
limited runs at their initial date of release. This practice
lay dormant throughout the sixties; however, it has been re-
vived in the seventies in the rock sector, particularly with
albums. Examples of this recent upsurge include a marble-
cake pattern for Dave Mason's *Alone Together* (Blue Thumb) and

red vinyl in the J. Geils Band's *Bloodshot* (Atlantic). Colored
plastic has come to be used more frequently among bootleg
recordings, primarily as a nostalgia item. A noteworthy example is a three-record set capturing the Wings Over America
1976 bicentennial tour. The discs here are successively red,
white, and blue.

Record labels of the fifties have also achieved a vogue
with collectors. The seventies have seen a proliferation of
imaginative designs far surpassing the logos employed by record companies in the fifties. Whereas the designs of the
fifties are useful primarily for identification purposes (i.e.,
so that consumers may avoid being duped by cleverly manufactured bootlegs), those of the seventies are valued more for
their aesthetic qualities. Some labels are unique to a given
release, such as the *Concert for Bangladesh* (Apple) which
showed a child affected by the famine in that country. These
extra features will probably exercise little influence in the
development of library collections concerned with day-to-day
usage. However, they may well be of value to certain archives
as objects of research or of intellectual curiosity.

A COMPARISON OF FORMATS

Once the particular sound recordings one wants to procure have
been decided upon, it is time to consider the type of format
best suited to the library's purposes. The major formats to
be considered for sound recordings are discs, cassette cartridge tapes, 8-track tapes, and open-reel tapes. There are
a number of more esoteric forms which have yet to gain widespread acceptance (or are now passe), including video tape
units (which combine a visual track along with the sound portion), wire tapes, cylinders, and piano rolls. The major place
for these formats at present is the research archives.

The leading formats each possess their own inherent advantages and disadvantages. An important advantage of the
tape formats over the disc has been the absence of pops, ticks,
scratches, etc., on a new product and the impossibility that
such defects would appear as a result of usage. However,
these examples of surface noise are neutralized in the case
of prerecorded tapes by the presence of high amounts of tape
hiss. And, although well produced homemade tape recordings
(particularly those emanating from a recorder employing a
Dolby unit) can overcome the problem of noticeably high levels
of hiss, these tapes are only as good as the records they have
been reproduced from. Another disadvantage of tapes is the
ever present danger of accidental erasure. This problem has
been overcome by prerecorded cassette manufacturers by means
of a certain plastic case configuration which renders it im-
possible to enable a new recording to be superimposed over
the old one. For users of blank tapes in each of the three
formats, the ability to erase recordings no longer wanted and
to make new ones in their place represents a highly desirable
characteristic. Sometimes unwanted erasure of a different
type can occur, as in the case of dropouts resulting from
aging of the tape or improper storage. The proneness of open-
reel tapes to stretching and breaking, as well as various
mechanical defects plaguing the housings of cassettes and
cartridges, represent additional problems for users.

With respect to tape recording, the library is possessed
of the opportunity to develop broader resource collections and
implement a far wider range of programs and activities in much
the same manner as commercial agencies such as radio and television. Unlike these commercial entities, however, the public
library is a nonprofit organization. While this implies the
freedom to attempt certain pioneering activities without the
necessity of reducing all considerations to a dollars-and-cents

quotient, it does not mean that the library can in any way
ignore the feasibility factor with respect to the development
of collections and programs. In this sense, it would make
little sense for the library to usurp those functions which
the library might be in a position to undertake more efficiently.
It is the responsibility of the library's public relations
apparatus to convince these agencies, as well as the general
public, that a symbiotic relationship could be worked out between them with regard to the recorded sound sector.

A chart comparing the advantages (and disadvantages) of,
say, the public library in relation to a given agency might be
drawn up around a particular type of service as a means of determining just what responsibilities the library is equipped
to handle most efficiently. An example can be found in Table
1 with respect to the tape recording of music by an individual
within the privacy of his home.

While the recording of tapes is vital to libraries for
the purposes of (a) providing extra copies and (b) acquiring
materials not available on either commercially recorded tapes
or discs, the prerecorded variety would seem to represent a
commodity less desirable than its equivalent on disc in view
of its following disadvantages:

1. Until 1977, prerecorded tapes were more expensive per
   unit than comparable phonorecords. The difference
   has been offset in the newer recordings by means of
   price standardization (i.e., $7.98 per unit); even-
   tually this development will cover older sound recordings as well.

2. They are vulnerable to accidental erasure.

3. They require monitoring to determine erasure or editing, whereas the disc can be judged to a great degree by means of inspection of the surface with the
   naked eye.

4. With respect to the open-reel variety, it is possible
   for the tape to be rewound on to another reel with
   the wrong end out.

TABLE 1   A comparison of the Advantages Offered by Two Agencies in Tape Recording: The Radio versus the Library

Advantages of the radio	Advantages of the library
1. A larger selection of materials to choose from (due to the promo records system).	1. The patron can select exactly what he wants, when he wants; less reliance upon the element of surprise.
2. The recordings are generally in better condition (because they are handled only by radio personnel and used on radio equipment).	2. No worry of a piece of music being incomplete due to (a) the programming taste of the disc jockey, (b) missing the opening portion while getting the tape recorder properly prepared for usage, and (c) sequi, a device in w which the disc jockey fades the music while talking over it, either at its beginning or ending.
3. Convenience. The enthusiast does not have to leave the confines of his home. Music can be selected at the flick of a dial.	
4. No worry about a piece of music being unavailable (i.e., checked out); everything in the radio station's library is ready to be played.	3. Objectivity. All materials present receive equal treatment. No recordings are emphasized to the exclusion of others.
5. Timeliness. New recordings are acquired more rapidly by radio stations, sometimes even before the official release date.	4. Less chance of outside interference while recording, e.g., static on the AM band, sudden dips in power on both AM and FM stations.

5.   They do not permit as convenient a selection of a cer-
     tain portion of the total product.

6.   They may stretch, curl, break, or lose quality in
     their sound reproduction if not carefully handled and
     stored. While they require an environment similar to
     that of discs for purposes of storage (i.e., a relative
     humidity of approximately 50 percent and a temperature
     of about 70°), tapes are far more likely to deteriorate
     through lack of use.

7. They are less famaliar to and, therefore, more diffi-
    cult for the average patron to handle. It remains a
    fact that considerably less people have tape recorders
    in comparison with owners of phonograph playback equip-
    ment.

8. Prerecorded tapes offer less variety of selection than
    is characteristic of phonorecords.

The advantages inherent in the use of tapes would appear
to represent ample justification for the selection of one of
these formats rather than discs in some cases. These advantages include:

1. The repairs of damaged tape are usually simple and
    quick.

2. On the more intricately constructed tape recorders one
    can superimpose new material upon an already existing
    recording; for example, spoken commentary, background
    music, sound effects, etc.

3. A recording can be easily altered by means of editing.

4. Recordings made privately on first-rate tape with a
    high-quality machine possess a higher degree of fi-
    delity than do discs.

5. Tape cannot be scratched although it is susceptable
    to other types of physical deterioration.

6. Tape provides greater versatility in that it can be
    reused when erased.

7. Tape is a space-saver in comparison with phonorecords;
    that is, more playing time can be fit on to a full
    reel. Many prerecorded tapes, however, include only
    a disc's worth of material on a reel; most of the reel
    is left empty.

Each of the three major tape formats has certain chara-
cterisitics which favor it over the other two types. Cassettes
are (a) the smallest in size, (b) the most versatile with
respect to freedom in carrying the equipment around, and,
(c) played on the least expensive machines. In short, they
provide the finest sound for the least expense. Eight-track
cartridges are the most convenient with regard to inserting

the tape and in the capability to enable the tape to play continually. Open-reel tapes provide the finest possible fidelity, ease in editing, and are capable of playing continually
if an expensive machine equipped with a "sensing strip" is
utilized. The key to choosing a particular tape format is to
determine first just what a given library's needs are going
to be.

The choice of what disc speed ought to receive priority
treatment would appear, at first glance, to represent a relatively easy process of decision making. The longplaying 33-
rpm disc has long been the preferred format in library collections. However, some libraries had developed extensive
holdings of 78's long before the advent of the LP. In that
a healthy portion of these old shellac discs have not been
reissued as longplaying albums, preservation of them would
seem a desirable policy. In addition to vintage performances
of the classics, many rare blues and jazz performances exist
only on 78's.

A similar situation can be found with respect to 45-rpm
discs. While almost all classical selections available in
this format were culled from albums, many valuable songs in
the popular, rhythm and blues, and rock fields have been released only on 45's. This argument goes in direct opposition
to the follwing advantages which can be derived from sticking
to one speed (i.e., 33 rpm):

1. The long-playing album is the source for most serious
    music as well as the bulk of all recorded literature.

2. It simplifies processing and shelving within the li-
    brary setting.

3. It necessitates fewer precautions and explanations
    aimed at library patrons.

4. The speed selector and stylus on library phonographs
    can be set for one speed.

5. Longplaying albums contain more material on one disc than is the case with any other speed; the result is one of optimum economy as well as increased convenience.

6. The quality of recorded sound is higher for 33-rpm discs than for any of the other speed formats.

As many reasons can be found for not including only longplaying albums within a library collection:

1. As noted earlier, certain recordings are not available on 33-rpm discs. In many cases, the balance of cuts from an album featuring an exceptionally good single (i.e., 45-rpm recording) may be so mediocre as to recommend acquisition of the 45 rather than the larger format.

2. "Talking books" and other nonmusical items are available at only the 16 2/3-rpm and 8 1/3-rpm speeds.

3. Some libraries will find the high cost of albums to be a prohibitive factor; rather the judicious selection of 45-rpm recordings would assist in keeping within budgetary allotments.

4. Albums can be unwieldy when searching for one particular cut on the side of a disc. Longplaying records are also harder to handle than the other formats.

5. Albums are less durable than 45's and 78's in some respects; that is, they are more likely to become scratched or warped.

6. Certain age groups prefer both the material available on as well as the physical character of 45's. The same was true of 78's in another time period.

In recognition of potential problems reflected in the above listing, it would appear that all speed formats ought to be considered for inclusion in library collections. 78's would be impractical for everyday circulation purposes; however, their archival value might be considerable. Additional copies could be reproduced onto tape in cases where open circulations or widespread research within the library setting are desirable.

The final format controversy was one which, for all practical purposes, was solved in the mid-sixties. At this time,
the monaural line was discontinued and stereo discs became
the norm. While mono records are no longer manufactured for
releases mastered in the studio with stereo equipment, they
are still being made for those works initially done with mono
machines. At one time, the general rule of thumb had been to
rechannel mono recordings so as to achieve "electronically
reproduced" stereo. The resulting sound was thin and crit-
icized by music purists as being unfaithful to the original
conditions of a given work as a conceptualized art form.
Therefore, there has been a movement back to the use of monaural in discs within both the classical and popular fields
where this was how the initial master was produced. On rare
occasions, contemporary artists still employ mono in order to
achieve a certain sound. An example of this is Dr. Feelgood's
Down By the Jetty (United Artists, 1975). This British group
sought to recapture the raucous, densely textured sound of
American rhythm and blues of the late fifties and early sixties.
Other subjects have also remained completely satisfactory in
a monophonic context (e.g., instructional material).

The playback of mono discs on stereo home equipment no
longer poses compatibility problems as it did some ten to fifteen years ago. The present-day industry has learned a valuable lesson from the past; it is reflected in the compatibility
between quadraphonic discs and tapes and stereo playback equipment.

AVAILABILITY OF THE RECORDING

The availability variable represents the last step in the process of acquiring records for libraries. Ultimately, it is
perhaps as important as the performance and reputation factors

in determining library acquisitions. Traditionally, the major
sources for library orders have been library jobbers and record
companies. The disadvantages of dealing directly with these
agencies are (a) the comparatively high costs entailed; (b)
the high risk of receiving defective recordings, and the at-
tendant problem of going about to achieve a satisfactory solution in the exchange in the exchange of these discs/tapes;
(c) the high rate of unavailable recordings listed in an up-
to-date copy of the *Schwann Monthly Catalog*; and (d) the long
waiting period characteristic of the time between placing an
order and receiving it.

Accordingly, a consideration of the other sources for obtaining recordings would seem to be in order. These sources
include the following:

1. Local wholesalers and retailers, the latter of which
   includes department store, mainstream record stores
   and specialized disc outlets. The advantages of pur-
   chasing recordings from such channels includes personalized advice from individuals who are oftentimes
   extremely knowledgeable on the subject and immediate
   access to the materials if in stock at that time.
   Usually the prices are competitive with those offered
   by jobbers and record companies direct.

2. Special mail order clubs. Many of these are operated
   by the major U.S. record label, e.g., Columbia, RCA,
   and Capitol. Columbia currently sponsors an institutional club geared towards libraries and similar public
   service organizations. Its weaknesses include a lack
   of selection control by the participating agency and a
   narrow field of choice; the catalog is predominantly
   represented by releases from its own stable of artists.
   The Record Club of America, which offered a wide variety of selections at sometimes more than 50 percent
   off retail cost upon the initial payment of a $5
   membership fee, represented a highly praised club until its demise in the early seventies. A present-day
   agency offering contemporary releases in all musical
   genres at very low prices is Record Source International,
   operated by Billboard Publishing Company. Monthly
   order sheets listing the best-selling albums in the

major stylistic categories of music are sent to interested institutions. The cost, as of December 1976,
was $1.98 per disc plus 25 cents handling and mailing
fees. This outlet has placed only one stipulation;
that a minimum of five albums per month be purchased.

3. Flea markets, auctions, porch sales, etc., provide
   an even cheaper avenue for the acquisition of recordings. The prime problem here is that of understanding
   enough about music and the care of records/tapes so
   as to be assured of achieving a sufficient return on
   one's investment. These sources often enable the
   buyer to buy up large amounts of recordings at one
   time.

4. Freebees, that is, promotional copies of records obtained either radio stations, reviewers, area record
   companies, or other well-to give promo discs to libraries of convinced of the usage and potential ad-
   vertising value which will follow out of such a practice. In the best interests of the library as a nonprofit agency, a "no strings attached" policy should
   be used in accepting such gifts.

5. Other libraries and people by means of taping recordings.
   Gifts from these sources represents another possible
   avenue for the acquisition of discs and tapes. Gifts
   are an excellent means of obtaining duplicates of
   popular discs; however, they should not be utilized
   to take the place of a regular budget. A key consideration here is that all recordings received as gifts
   must meet the criteria outlined for selection. The
   public-relations apparatus plays an important role in
   drumming up activity for the gifts sector. The quality
   of past service characterizing a library can have a
   strong influence on the amount of gifts coming in.

6. A more controversial channel is that of bootleg recordings, i.e., discs or tapes recorded illegally and
   manufactured without the sanction of the companies
   owning the contract rights to the artist in question.
   The sources of these bootlegs include retail outlets,
   mail order direct from the labels themselves, and
   personally manufactured discs and tapes. The major
   problem in dealing with bootlegs is the obvious ethics
   issue. Is it right to deprive companies which made a
   financial investment in artists of their deserved roy-
   alties? The artists add to this, complaining that
   many of these recordings are poor from a technical
   standpoint and often catch them at something less than
   their best. The argument propounded by most purchasers

of bootleg recordings is that the record companies and
artists themselves have done music enthusiasts an extreme disservice by not making certain recordings
(usually of live performances) available to the public
through commercial channels. They rarely fail to
mention that they own all the official releases by a
particular artist; therefore, the purchase of bootleg
recordings is in no way subtracting from the profits
potentially to be had by either the record company or
the artist. The appearance of foreign recordings only
serves to further complicate the copyright issue sur-
rounding bootlegging. Obviously, libraries must exercise intelligence and tact in dealing with this emo-
tionally charged issue. On one side we have the goal
of providing the fullest possible range of recordings
for the public; on the other hand, it is not in best
interests of librarians to erode whatever good will
exists between themseleves and commercial agencies
concerned with the recorded sound industry.

POTENTIAL FOR CIRCULATION

The circulation figures expected of a given sound recording in
the future should not be the sole consideration in the selection process. Rather, librarians would be wise to chosse from
a pool of recordings designated as possessing a high projected
circulation rate those discs and tapes deemed to have the
finest aesthetic, socially astute, etc., qualities. Indicators
of the potential for library usage include (a) the bestselling
charts, (b) radio playlists, (c) informal polls of the tastes
of one's clientele, (d) reviews, (e) an artist's past track
record, and (f) the publicity generated by a given artist.
Certain types of libraries will be paying greater attention
to the popularity factor than others. However, cases are sure
to exist within each type of library setting in which recordings
will be acquired despite the fact that they are not expected
to be used widely.

   Librarians who feel unsure of themselves with regard to
the selection of sound recordings may choose to follow these

guidelines on a systematic point-by-poing basis. It is this
author's belief that some librarians may already be employing
an internalized variation of this scheme with great success.

Chapter 3

ANNOTATED LISTING OF PERIODICALS TO BE USED
IN THE SELECTION PROCESS

INTRODUCTION

A vast number of periodicals dealing with music and/or sound
recordings are currently available either on newsstand or
through the mail. This annotated compilation excludes those
which are not primarily concerned with one of these two inter-
related areas. Extreme differences in editorial purpose,
writing style, and quality of coverage can be found to characterize the titles below. The sole consideration in their inclusion has been whether they in some way contribute to the
librarian's reservoir of knowledge about sound recordings,
thereby enabling him to more perceptively assess the available
releases.

THE ALPHABETIZED LIST

Acid Rock. Dave Fass, Editor-in chief. Stories , Layouts, &
Press, New York, 1977-. Bimonthly. Rate: $1.50/issue.

  Acid Rock attempts to fill a void in today's music periodical field which has existed for some time, i.e., the ab-

sence of a publication concerned totally with the psychedilic
sounds which originally evolved into a definable entity in the
mid-sixties. While many of the articles are genuinely informative, the overall effectiveness of the magazine is undermined
by journalistic excess based upon unabashed hero worship and
sophomoric stabs of hip subculture humor. The format is attractive; an abundance of photographs is present, including
approximately one-half dozen color pinups per issue. There
are not any record reviews in *Acid Rock,* although both books
and concerts are covered. A balance is sought between historical analysis and commentary dealing with the current scene.
American Record Guide (incorporating the American Tape Guide).
James Lyons, Editor. American Record Guide, New York, 1934-.
Monthly.

American Record Guide attempts to provide comprehensive
coverage of classical recordings via the review format. Recordings of the same work are often compared and two reviewers
will occasionally set forth differing opinions with regard to
a given recording. Jazz is briefly covered, as is hi-fi equipment. Each issue features the study of an important artist's
work; scholarly discographical compilations are included as
well.
Billboard The International Music-Record Newsweekly. Leo Zhito,
Editor. Billboard, Cincinnati, 1894-. Weekly. Rate $1.75/is-
sue.

This glossy-paged tabloid is aimed primarily at those commercial entrepreneurs concerned with the publishing, recording,
and retailing of music. It is also of inestimable value to
those interested in viewing the music industry from the inside.
Included are news items covering almost everything having to
do with the performing and/or recording of music, best-selling
record charts for all major genres, concert itineraries, di-
rectories of music publishing firms and booking agents, etc.

The record and tape releases for a given work are listed here, making *Billboard* a valuable bibliographic tool. Record reviews are rarely longer than a few sentences in length and take the form of advertisements aimed at retailers rather than discriminating critiques.

Bim Bam Boom. Steve Flam and Ralph Newman, Editors. Bim Bam Boom Enterprises, New York, Bimonthly. Rate: $1.50/issue.

Bim Bam Boom is devoted to the historical analysis of rhythm and blues music of the fifties and sixties. The articles are well written and usually include a large number of attractive photographs--both of which are rarities for a specialized music periodical of this nature. *Bim Bam Boom* is the only journal concerned primarily with rhythm and blues music which utilizes a glossy-stock format; the other two publications at the fore in this area, *Record Exchanger* and *Yesterday's Memories,* employ a text with unadjusted margins upon a much cheaper grade of paper.

Blues & Soul Music Review.[2] John E. Abbey, Editor. Contempo International, London, Biweekly. Rate: $6.50/issue. (Originally *Who Put the Bomp.*)

Perhaps the finest journal ever published concerned with the rock music scene, past and present. Its breadth is astounding; the past half-dozen issues include articles covering the British Invasion, punk rock, Beatle novelties, rockabilly, surfing music, girl groups, surveys of Dutch and Swedish rock, and interviews with Brian Wilson and arranger Jack Nitzsche. An equally impressive array of regular columns are present in *Bomp,* including editorials, fan letters, news briefs, and reviews of books, fanzines, singles, and albums. The writing is professional and highly astute with respect to its level of aesthetic analysis and sociological commentary. The records reviewed tend to be rather obscure; they rarely receive attention anywhere else in the periodical literature. The format

is extremely attractive considering the fact that *Bomp* appeals
to something of a cult audience. Glossy-stock paper featuring
a healthy assortment of black-and-white photos is used. Discographies are often appended to the articles.

Circus. Gerald Rothberg, Publsiher and Editor-in-chief. Circus Enterprises, New York, Biweekly. Rate: $12.00/year; $1.00/
issue.

  Circus attempts to capture that audience of serious rock
music enthusiasts still too young (under twenty-one) to fully
appreciate the coverage in *Rolling Stone*. *Circus* employs glossy paper with profuse illustrations in its endeavors to chronicle popular culture developments on a wide variety of fronts,
including the cinema, television, and contemporary issues and
phenomena (e.g., birth control, jogging, politics). Also present are a balanced array of regular departments such as short
news notes ("Front Pages"), "Letters," "Into Your Head" (which
features a psychoanalyst's advice to teenagers with problems
of various types), a concert timetable, and a reader's poll of
favorite albums. The record reviews are both authoritative
and lucidly written, while not as intellectually complex as
those appearing in *Rolling Stone*.

Contemporary Keyboard. Tom Darter, Editor. GPI, Saratoga,
Calif., 1975-. Monthly. Rate: $12.00/year; $1.00/issue.

  This journal features a format identical to that of *Guitar
Player*. The articles are serious in tone, usually centering
around an interview with a keyboardist in one of various musical genres (e.g., jazz, rock, blues, country, and classical).
Much attention is paid to matters of technique. As is the case
with *Guitar Player,* the record reviews are excellent. They
tend to focus upon the keyboard playing to a greater extent
than they do the overall musical qualities of the disc.

Country Music Review. Bryan Chalker, Editor. Hanover Books,
London, 1972-. Monthly. Rate: Ŀ2.59/year.

This journal provides an in-depth look at the country and western music field. The articles are serious in tone. Reviews of current releases are authoritative and lucidly written.

Country Music. KPO, New York. Monthly. Rate: $8.95/year; $1.00/issue.

Country Music follows roughly the same format within the Country and Western field as is characteristic of *Circus* in the rock sector, reviews, news briefs and gossip, feature stories, and correspondence all appear on a regular basis amidst an abundance of color illustrations. Although much space is devoted to hard-core country artists such as Loretta Lynn and George Jones, the magazine is strongly inclined in the direction of musicians possessed of rock-culture associations. The record review section in each issue includes only several albums; however, they are more lengthy and authoritative than those appearing in *Country Style,* its major rival in mass-circulation sweepstakes.

Country Music World. Dodson, Arlington, Va. 1972-. Rate: $5.95/year.

Another excellent publication attempting to chronicle the changing country and western scene. Available only through the mail or at shops specializing in this genre.

Country Style. Vince Sorren, Editor. Country Style, Franklin Park, Ill. 1976-. Biweekly. Rate: $13.00/year; $1.00/issue.

The title of this periodical is somewhat misleading in that a large portion of *Country Style* is given over to coverage of rock performers. For example, the August 25, 1977 issue includes articles on Steve Miller, the Eagles, Bobbie Gentry, and the Everly Brothers, as well as pop stars Tom Jones and Englebert Humperdinck. The format is similar to the majority of rock magazines; that is, besides articles, regular departments such as record reviews, news briefs, and letters from the readers appear here. Although the reviews are relatively short

in length, they are lucidly written and feature perceptive
critical assessments. Despite its having been printed on cheap
pulp, the format is considerably enhanced by an abundance of
photographs.

Crawdaddy examines the rock scene on a level closer to that of
the adult perspective taken by *Rolling Stone* than the teenage
approach emplyed by *Circus* and *Creem*. It attempts to chronicle
and analyze the cultural significance not only of the rock music arena, but politics, literature, and personalities of
other media as well. The early issues of *Crawdaddy* were printed
on cheap newspaper sheets; however, the journal now appears on
glossy stock and includes a large number of attractive color
photographs. The record reviews are of fairly extensive length
and are authoritative in treatment.

Creem. Barry Kramer, Editor. Creem, Birmingham, Mich. 1969-.
Monthly. Rate: $1.00/issue.

The punk mentality rules supreme in *Creem's* cosmos of priorities. The sophomoric humor and worship of dumbness which
permeate its pages will be hard for readers over eighteen years
of age to appreciate or identify with. However, the journal's
bias in favor of hard rock artists and preoccupation with the
counterculture ethic render it a gold mine of information for
those concerned with the interests of the audience whose tastes
Creem has attempted to satisfy. When reading the record reviews librarians have to keep in mind that their authoritative-
ness is subject to question; that is, the reviewers often
appear to be pandering for a laugh and tend to be obscure in
their allusions to other sources. The reviews often dispense
with a to-the-point analysis of the music itself. The articles
are frequently more straight forward and informative in their
treatment of artists and other related topics.

Discoworld. Transamerican, New York. Monthly. Rate $8.00/
year; $1.00/issue.

Discoworld attempts to exhaustively chronicle the disco scene; its music, personalities, fashions, and more. The magazine is lavishly illustrated and employs a fanzine approach with respect to its journalistic style. One issue in 1977 included a history of disco music, a listing of discotheques throughout the United States, a primer for beginning dancers, and tips on what to wear at the disco, in addition to features devoted to over half a dozen leading performers and disc jockeys in this area. Record reviews are short and decidely to-the-point; those readers desiring more in-depth and astute analysis of these recordings are advised to search out copies of *Rolling Stone, Melody Maker,* and *Soul.*

Down Beat. Dan Morgenstern, Editor. Maher, Chicago, 1934-. Monthly. Rate: $1.00/issue.

Down Beat is the most widely read jazz music journal in the entire world. Its level of writing is very high, both with respect to the feature articles and reviews. The latter include concerts and books in addition to recordings. *Down Beat* has managed to cultivate new readers interested in contemporary trends such as jazz-rock and disco, while satisfying the inclinations of the old guard desiring coverage of the performers, clubs, etc., related to the purist strains such as swing, bop, and cool jazz.

Gig. Gig, New York. Monthly. Rate: $7.97/year; $.85/issue.

Gig follows essentially the same format as that characterizing *Phonograph Record Magazine.* This monthly tabloid features wide-ranging coverage of the multi-faceted rock scene. The record reviews are competent; singles are covered as well as albums. Top-forty chart listings for both soul and rock music albums and singles are included.

Goldmine. Arena, Fraser, Mich. Monthly.

Goldmine bills itself as the "world's largest record collector's marketplace." A good deal of space is given over to

ads citing the records which various dealers and retailers
wish to either buy or sell. The tabloid also contains articles,
disographies, and reviews (Of both old and new recordings) on
a regular basis. Although the thythm and blues rarities of
the fifties tend to fetch the highest prices, discs of virtually every genre imaginable are liable to turn up in the
listings as published in *Goldmine*.

Guitar Player. Jim Grockett, Editor. Eastman, San Jose, Cal.
1967-. Monthly. Rate: $11.00/year; $1.00/issue.

Gives advice on how to develop musicians' skills, tests
and evaluates equipment, and provides concise and articulate
articles on guitarists in all musical genres. The record review section is small but authoritative. Both reviews and
articles assume some knowledge of the instrument.

High Fidelity. Roland Gelatt, Editor. Billboard, New York,
1951-. Monthly. Rate: $7.98/year; $1.00/issue.

High Fidelity is roughly similar in format to *Stero Review*.
Perhaps the major difference between the two magazines is that
the former has been less responsive to the rumblings within
the former has been less responsive to the rumblings within
the popular music sphere. Classical music has continued to
receive the greatest amount of space, both with respect to
feature articles and record reviews. The various popular music genres such as folk, jazz, and rock, however, have recently begun to garner additional attention within all sectors of
the journal. The record reviews are intelligently written,
although lacking the engaging style and convenient three-point
basis of evaluation characterizing those in *Stereo Review*.
High Fidelity pioneered the brief summary type of review which
has appeared in a multitude of other magazines of late.

Hit Parader. Lisa Robinson, Editor. Charlton, Derby, Conn.,
1954-. Monthly. Rate: $7.50/year; $.75/issue.

Hit Parader has been the definitive pop music mouthpiece
for teenagers during the past two decades. For this duration
it has attempted to provide intelligent yet accessible coverage of the rock scene for that age group devoid of the
journalistic sensationalism characterizing fanzines and counterculture journals. The record reviews are somewhat sophomoric
in approach, but probably succeed in their aim of hitting
home to youth. Each issue contains the lyrics to roughly three
dozen songs; the inclusion of a wealth of articles, new notes,
and correspondance renders *Hit Parader* the best pick of the
Charlton Family of music publications.

Jazz Journal. Sinclair Traill, Editor. Novello, London, 1948.
Monthly. Rate: Ł3.75/year.

Europeans have tended to be a step ahead of their New
World counterparts in an appreciation of indigenous American
music forms as high art. *Jazz Journal* is one of the best periodicals from abroad devoted to the serious study of jazz music. The reviews are lengthy and highly authoritative.

Journal of Popular Culture. Ray Browne, Editor. Popular Cul-
ture Association, Modern Language Association, and Midwest
Modern Language Association, Bowling Green, Ohio, 1967-.
Quarterly. Rate: $15.00/year; $4.00/issue.

The *Journal of Popular Culture* is devoted to the scholarly
analysis of popular culture in the broadest definition of that
term; that is, including sports, the women's suffrage movement,
changing attitudes on the part of the general public toward
Big Business, and political corruption, among other things.
On occasion, various popular music genres comprise the major
interest of a feature article. These articles are usually
fairly extensive in length and can be characterized as having
strong sociological underpinnings. They can be of much assistance in developing a collection of sound recordings, despite
the conspicuous absence of a reviewing format.

Listening Post. Caroline Saheb-Ettaba, Editor of final issue
(June 1976). Bro-Dart, City of Industry, Calif., 1970-76.
11 issues per year, plus cumulative issue appearing each July.
    In its own words, the journal

> is a guide to new recordings from domestic and
> foreign record companies, and is designated to
> assist librarians, teachers, and record collectors
> in the selection of recorded material. Each issue
> lists newly released discs and cassettes in all
> fields of interest: children's, spoken, documentary,
> languages, instructional, classical music, sound-
> tracks, and every variety of popular music, both
> traditional and contemporary. All available de-
> scriptive and bibliographic information is provided
> for each recording.

Also included is a listing of reviews from a number of leading
music periodicals under the heading of each recording which
appears in *Listening Post.* An order form, along with a guide
to its use, has been included in each issue for those recordings which are reviewed. The discounts offered here are
not particularly good; that is, 37 percent off list price for
albums and 20 percent off for cassettes. The reviewers, most
of whom are practicing librarians, are not very perceptive in
their analysis of the recording; some are downright silly.
Still, back issues remain valuable for purposes of retrospective
selection. The journal has been superseded by a title listing/
specification/order form which is issued monthly to interested
individuals and institutions free of charge.
Living Blues. Living Blues, Chicago, Bimonthly. Rate: $1.00/
issue.

    Living Blues is devoted to rendering blues a vital living
art form, both in its acoustic and electric variants. Historical as well as contemporary topics are covered in the journal.
The analysis characterizing the articles and reviews is of a
very high order.

Melody Maker. Ray Coleman, Editor. IPC Specialist and Professional, London, 1925-. Weekly. Rate: $39.00/year; $.75/
issue (U.S.A.)

   Melody Maker is a weekly tabloid covering the British popular music scene. Record reviews comprise a fairly large section
within the journal, including subdivisions into rock/pop albums,
jazz albums, folk albums, short commentaries on albums, and a
column devoted to the newest singles releases. *Melody Maker*
also includes a wide selection of feature articles as well as
regular contributions. The regular sections include British
and American best-seller charts, readers' mail, concert reviews and itineraries, and American news items. The articles
are frequently written well enough to rise above the typical
news reporting format; many of the issues include provocative
themes which encompass several articles (e.g., guitar virtuos-
ity, a survey of studio production in rock recordings). Both
the reviews and articles are lengthy and authoritative.

*Modern Recording Serving Today's Music/Recording-conscious
Society.* H.G. LaTorre, Editor. Cowan, Port Washington, N.Y.,
1976-. Monthly. Rate: $1.50/issue.

   Modern Recording emphasizes the technical side of making
music, both live and in the studio. Articles often focus upon how to employ complex electronic equipment relating to
either performing or the recording of music. Another frequent
inclusion is that of an interview with the engineer or producer of some recording act of note. The record review section
features expert analysis within the pop, jazz, and classical
fields.

Music and Letters. Denis Arnold and Edward Olleson, Editors.
Oxford University Press, London, 1920-. Quarterly. Rate:
Ł1.50/issue; Ł5.50/year.

   The journal is devoted to academic research in the field
of classical music. Stylistically, it is similar in approach

to *The Musical Quarterly;* however, *Music and Letters* differs
from the Schirmer publication insofar as its articles concentrate upon the music history of Great Britain and tend to avoid
all but the literary aspects of musicology. The review sections,
which cover only books and music scores, are authoritative and
exhaustive with respect to the nature of their commentary.

Music Journal. Hannah Hanani, Editor. Elemo, Southampton,
1943-. 10issues per year. Rate: $11.00/year.

The spotlight in *Music Journal* is upon classical music.
The articles usually are concerned with leading musicians and
conductors; either as a study of their respective lives and
music or in providing advice to students with respect to musical technique. Special features such as "An Index to the
Music Schools and Conservatories of the United States" are
also included on an occasional basis. The record reviews are
organized as a flowing commentary in two sections (classical
and jazz) with a short amount of space devoted to each recording.
Reviews and articles both feature a spare, lucid style of jour-
nalism. Attractive format.

The Musical Quarterly. Joan Peyser, Editor. Schirmer, New
York, 1915-. Quarterly. Rate: $14.00/year; $4.00/issue.

The articles of this journal are of a scholarly nature,
covering both contemporary and historical topics relating to
serious music. In their own words "special attention is paid
to biographical and analytical studies of twentiety-century
composers." The articles are often concerned with miniscule
topics; for example, a 1977 issue included "The Bass Part in
Haydn's Early String Quartets" and "Turkish Affect in the Land
of the Sun King." The journal is a valuable bibliographic tool
in that it contains a listing of relevant books published in
Europe and the United States in each issue. The reviews, concerned with books and music scores as well as records, are expertly written and feature rather lengthy text.

The Nashville Gospel. J. Nebraska Gifford, Editor. Nashville/ Gospel, New York, 1971-. Monthly. Rate: $10.00/year; $1.00/ issue.

This journal possesses a somewhat misleading title. It concentrates upon the family at a grass-roots level rather than exclusive coverage of the gospel music genre. The articles included cover family budgeting, religion, household improvements, and the wholesome aspects of the entertainment business. Country pop comprises the bulk of the music coverage. The record reviews each consist of a brief paragraph. The analysis is not particularly critical in these reviews; they could be better characterized as industry pronouncements.

New Musical Express. Tony Stewart, Editor. IPC, London, Weekly. Rate: $1.10/issue (U.S.); $.60/issue (Canada).

While both the contents and physical appearance of this tabloid are similar to that of *Melody Maker*, it provides a point of view heavily imbued with the counterculture ethic. Feature articles are highly informative, concentrating upon pop music events and developments within Great Britain (nevertheless, American artists and music are covered extensively as well). Record reviews are also excellent; they are slightly more comprehensive than those in *Melody Maker*. The charts provide an interesting sidelight; besides the best-selling surveys for albums and singles in the United Kingdom and United States, the top ten singles in England five, ten, and fifteen years ago are also lsited.

Notes. Harold E. Samuel, Editor. Music Library Association, School of Music, University of Michigan, Ann Arbor, 1943-. Quarterly.

Notes represents one of the finest bibliographic tools available to librarians with respect to the coverage of sound recordings. Although several scholarly articles concerned with music research appear in each issue, the major emphasis

of the journal is upon book and record reviews. Of particular
value to the record librarian will be the consensus record
review, which covers hundreds of discs and provides an index
function for reviews in other music publications. Listings
of books and recordings received are also included. The pre-
dominant interest here is in classical music.

Opera. Harold Rosenthal, Editor. Seymour, London, 1950-.
Monthly. Rate: Ł8.75/year.

   Opera is one of the definitive journals concerned with the
analysis of this art form. Reviews of both recordings and
performances are first-rate. Its coverage is international
in scope.

Opera News. Frank Merkling, Editor. Metropolitan Opera Guild,
New York, 1936-. Irregular (during opera season); Monthly
(rest of year)

   Opera News is the most influential periodical concerned
with opera published in the United States. The issues published during the Metropolitan Opera season showcase the work
that is presently being performed. The monthly installments
concern themselves more with the historical development and
significant composers, performers, etc., of opera. Short news
reports of musical activities which are international in scope
appear as a regular department. Concise, authoritative record reviews concerning important opera and vocal releases
also are included in each issue.

Paul's Record Magazine. Paul Bezanker, Editor. Paul E.
Bezanker, Hartford, Bimonthly. Rate: $5.00/year; $1.00/issue.

   One of the best fanzines concerned with chronicling the
history of rock and roll. What it lacks in physical appearance
(typewritten pages reproduced by mimeograph) and polished
writing, *PRM* more than makes up for in enthusiasm and the ten-
acious search for newsworthy features. Much space is devoted
to interviews with music personalities from the past and the

listing of discographical data. Some articles, however, amount
to meaningless filler (e.g., one issue contains a running commentary on the WWGM Top 40 for the week of Novermber 10, 1957).
Of particular interest to those institutions emphasizing collections in fifties rhythm and blues. Auction notices for old
discs are included.

Phonograph Record Magazine. Bob Fukuyama, Editor. Phonograph
Record, Hollywood, Calif., Monthly. Rate: $7.50/year; $.75/
issue.

    Phonograph Record Magazine represents a watered down al-
ternative to *Rolling Stone.* Available free of charge to cus-
tomers at selected retail record outlets across the country,
the periodical attempts to provide intelligent coverage of
the rock and soul music scenes without the spicy counterculture overtones displayed by Wenner's tabloid. Both the articles and record reviews tend to be overly congratulatory
rather than objectively critical of a given artist's work.
Almost one-half of the magazine is devoted to jazz and soul
music.

Record Exchanger. Art Turco, Editor. Vintage Records, Anaheim,
Calif., 1969. Bimonthly. Rate: $1.50/issue.

    As in the case of *Bim Bam Boom* and *Yesterday's Memories,*
Record Exchanger is devoted to documenting the history of fifties rhythm and blues. Most articles include lengthy discographies relating to the artists covered. Price listings
of both individual collectors and retailers comprise an extensive prtion of the journal. *Record Exchanger* also publishes
a record catalog on an annual basis which functions as a cumulative edition of these listings.

Record Reviews. Brian J. Ashley, Editor and Publisher.
Ashley Communications, Los Angeles, Calif., 1977-. Bimonthly.
Rate: $6.00/year; $1.00/issue.

This journal represent something of a librarian's dream
with respect to the evaluation and selection of records.
Record Reviews is comprised completely of reviews; they are
generally extensive in length and authoritative in treatment.
They cover the entire span of music genres, including rock,
country and western, jazz, folk, and classical. One drawback
is that the inclusions here are by no means comprehensive in
scope. The magazine has been printed on high-quality stock
paper and the presence of numerous illustrations contribute
to its overall appeal.

Right On! Cynthia Horner, Editor. Laufer, Hollywood, Calif.,
Monthly. Rate: $7.00/year; $.75/issue.

Like *Circus, Right On!* attempts to appeal to mature teenagers; however, it concerns itself with covering the soul music scene rather than mainstream rock as in the case of the
former. The magazine includes within its pages articles and
news notes in addition to regular features such as reviews,
record charts, and letters to the editor. The visual aspect
of *Right On!* is extremely attractive, including an abundance
of photographs (many of which are in color).

Rock and Soul Songs. Lisa Robinson, Editor. Charlton, Derby,
Conn. Monthly. Rate: $7.50/year; $.75/issue.

Song Hits Magazine. William T. Anderson, Executive editor.
Charlton, Derby, Conn. Monthly. Rate: $5.00/year; $.50/
issue.

Both of these Charlton publications are geared toward an
early teen (or younger) audience. *Song Hits Magazine* is devoted almost entirely to the reproduction in print form of
pop, soul, and country tune lyrics. These listings should
be an important guideline for librarians in ascertaining those
songs possessing words which might render them deserving of
inclusion in library collections. The only other inclusion
in this periodical is that of one feature article apiece for

the pop, soul, and country music genres, respectively.

Rock and Soul Songs deviates from this format slightly insofar as it contains (brief) news items and short articles
as a complement to the listings of rock and soul song lyrics.
The textual material covers personalities in the television
and movie fields as well as those belonging to the popular music scene. A fairly large degree of duplication exists between
these two magazines with respect to soul and rock song lyrics;
therefore, it would appear to be unnecessary to purchase them
both.

Rock Scene. Richard Robinson, Editor. Four Seasons, Bethany,
Conn., 1973-. Bimonthly. Rate: $4.00/year.

A widely circulated magazine which attempts to reach essentially the same audience as that of *Circus* and *Creem*.
Coverage is competant, although not up to the standards set
by *Crawdaddy* and *Rolling Stone*.

Rockingchair. John Politis, Editor. Cupola, Philadelphia,
1977-. Monthly. Rate: $6.95/year (for librarians); $11.95/
year (for others).

This newsletter attempts to cultivate an understanding of
popular-music recordings on the part of librarians. *Rockingchair* reviews popular music of all types, emphasizing the artistic merits and potential usage by library patrons. The
publication also analyzes sheet music and folios, provides
advice on record care, discusses ways of promoting and circulating discs, and reviews discographical publications.

Rolling Stone. Jann S. Wenner, Editor and Publisher. Rolling
Stone, New York, 1967-. Biweekly. Rate: $18.00/year; $1.00/
issue.

Rolling Stone has remained, since its inception, the pre-
mier publication covering the popular music field. However,
it is far more than a music journal. Although rock has always been its bread and butter, it provides an astute commentary

upon world politics and popular culture studies in general.
Feature articles are extremely lengthy, sometimes entailing
more than twenty pages of a newspaper tabloid format. A large
number of regularly appearing columns are included in *Rolling
Stone,* including "Grandstand" (a serious commentary on virtually
any topic imaginable with strong sociological underpinnings),
"Random Notes," "Caught Live," and "Political News." The
record reviews represent one of the journal's true strengths;
they are generally objective and feature highly intelligent
analysis, despite an inclination to put down more middle-of-
the-road music aspirations. In short, just about anything of
note happening in the American pop music scene makes an appearance in its pages.

Schwann Catalog. Schwann, Boston. Monthly. Rate: $1.00/issue.

   The *Schwann Catalog* represents the definitive bibliograph-
ical tool devoted to the field of sound recordings. It comprehensively lists all records currently in the classical,
pop/rock, jazz, and show and soundtrack music genres. The
popular and jazz genres are organized by artist, whereas
classical music is by composer and show and soundtrack music
by title. A semiannual supplement lists all tape releases
and older pop records known to be in print. The entries themselves are brief, including in all categories the delineation
of artist, title, record label (accompanied by the company's
assigned number), list price, and month of release. The
Schwann Catalog will not assist librarians in the evaluation
process. Rather, its purpose will be that of revealing just
what recordings are available for selection in various fields
and the artists producing them.

Shmoozin. Integrity, New York, 1977-. Weekly. Distributed
free at selected record outlets nationwide.

Shmoozin is a tasty little sampler (under twenty-five
pages in length) which aims at providing a little of something
for music enthusiasts of all types. Feature articles frequently concentrate upon up-and-coming or cult artisits. The
record reviews, which are divided between rock and classical
album releases and the latest pop singles, function as brief
descriptive pronouncements rather than acutely analytical
critiques. *Record World's* "Album Chart," representing the
nation's top 100 LP's as compiled by the editors of that journal on a wwekly basis, has been reproduced here. An added
benefit, other than finding out what America buys, is the presence of basic discographical information as well as the manu-
facturer's list price for each disc within this chart. The
brief music news column approach popularized by publications
such as *Rolling Stone* and *Crawdaddy* is also included in
Shmoozin.
Sing Out. Irwin Silber, Editor. Sing Out, New York, 1950-.
Bimonthly. Rate: $1.00/issue.
This journal is the bible of folk scene. It employs a
strong scholarly bent in the analysis of artists, the development of certain songs, and folk instruments such as the banjo,
Autoharp, and dulcimer. Although the record reviews are excellent, the major thrust of *Sing Out* is upon the spontaneous
making of music, that is, folk artistry. Included with this
aim in mind are interviews which feature both traditional and
contemporary folk personalities as well as the words, music,
and guitar chords to a number of folk songs in each issue.
16. Randi Reisfeld, Editor. 16 Magazines, New York. Monthly.
Rate: $7.00/year; $.60/issue.
16 employs roughly the same format as is present in fanzines
such as *Teen Favorites* and *Tiger Beat.* The coverage is pre-
occupied with trivial and extramusical detail; critical analysis is rarely, if ever, present. Photographs are attractive

and abundant, featuring movie and television stars as well as
musicians.

Soul. Regina Nickerson Jones, Editor. Soul, Los Angeles,
Biweekly. Tate: $7.00/year; $.50/issue.

This periodical is one of the most informative organs devoted to coverage of the soul music field. Utilizing a tabloid format, *Soul* offers competantly written feature articles
and record reviews. A good buy in view of its low price.

Soul Sounds. Rod Bristow, Editor. Albuc, New York, 1973-.
Monthly. Rate: $5.99/year.

While coming dangerously close to being a teenybopper fanzine, *Soul Sounds* represents one of the richest sources of information relating to developments in this genre. The format
is attractive, employing the same mixture of feature articles
and regular columns, extras, etc., characterizing most pop music publications of a mass-circulation variety.

Stereo Review. William Anderson, Editor. Ziff-Davis, New
York, 1958-. Monthly. Rate: $7.98/year; $1.00/issue.

Stereo Review aims at appealing to the discriminating high-
fidelity enthusiast possessed of an equally perceptive ear
for music. The format is divided between an analysis of equipment and sound recordings in all musical genres. The review
section is very exhaustive in length, featuring coverage of
tapes as well as discs. They are judged according to three
major criteria: performance, recording, and stereo quality.
The articles are frequently well-researched and generously
appended with illustrations. They tend to highlight either
composers or artists of current interest or provocative themes
such as why women have rarely excelled as composers of serious
music. A must in all libraries.

Superteen. Kathy Loy, Editor. Sterling's Magazines, New York.
Monthly. Rate: $12.00/year; $1.00/issue.

Superteen follows a predictable teen fan-magazine mold; that is, it includes many pinup pictures, the so-called "inside" information as to what a given musician likes and dislikes, and contests in which the reader can win prizes relating to his or her fondest fantasies. Also present are (a) a correspondance section, (b) advice to teenagers about their problems, (c) news items, (d) articles, and (e) short reviews of an informative rather than a critical nature. As in the case of other fan magazines, television and cinema are covered as well as pop musicians. While the articles and reviews in periodicals of this type are of little value in assisting librarians to make the best choices as to what belongs in their collections, they do serve an invaluable function in acquainting librarians with what youth like and why they like it.

Teen Bag. Lillian Smith, Editor. Lopez, New York. 1977-. Monthly. Rate: $9.00/year; $.75/issue.

This periodical is somewhat less musically oriented than most fanzines aiming for an audience in its early teens. Despite its superficial coverage, *Teen Bag* is of value as a document of the tastes of youth.

Teen Favorites. Richard Lewis, Editor. Cousins, New York, 1977-. Monthly. Rate: $15.00/year; $1.25/issue.

Teen Favorites is aimed at a preteen audience. It features movie and television personalities as well as popular music stars. It is more valuable as a guide to the tastes of young people than it is as a discriminating medium concerned with pop music.

Tempo A Quarterly Review of Modern Music. David Drew, Editor-in-chief. Regent, London. Quarterly. Rate: $2.00/issue.

Tempo is devoted to the composers, works, and history of music in the twentiety centry. The journal is scholarly in tone, and includes reviews of books, performances, and records. The record reviews are expertly written, featuring indepth analysis of the serious music genre.

Tiger Beat. Sheila Murphy, Editor. Laufer, Hollywood, Calif., 1977-. Bimonthly. Rate: $5.00/year; $1.00/issue.

   Tiger Beat is similar to *Teen Favorites* in that it employs a fanzine approach to its coverage of the entertainment scene and employs an abundance of colorful photographs geared toward the under-thirteen audience.

Trans-Oceanic Trouser Press. Trans-Oceanic Trouser, New York. Bimonthly. Rate: $1.50/issue.

   Trans-Oceanic Trouser Press is concerned with the British rock from the early sixties up to the present. The journal parleys in a hip commentary style reminiscent of *Rolling Stone* and the text is interspersed with an abundance of illustrations. Record reviews and discographies occupy a prominant place in this magazine. The reviews concentrate upon the most recent releases; however, older recordings are frequently analyzed in the feature articles.

Variety. Variety, New York. Weekly. Rate: $3.00/year; $.75/issue.

Cash Box. Gary Cohen, Editor-in-chief. Cash Box, New York. Weekly. Rate: $70.00/year.

Record World. Sid Parnes, Editor. Record World, New York. Weekly.

   Each of these journals follows roughly the same format as is utilized in *Billboard*. All except *Record World* attempt to comprehensively cover the show business field; important financial dealings, the latest developments in the careers of important performers, etc. They each carry their own record charts and review sections. As in the case of *Billboard,* the reviews tend to function more as industry pronouncements than as serious critiques on a given recording's artisitic merits.

Yesterday's Memories. Marsha Vance, Marv Goldberg, and Mike Redmond, Editors, Freebizak, New York, 1975-76. Bimonthly

Rate: $3.50/4 issues; $1.00/issue; $2.00/issue in foreign countries.

Although no longer in print, *Yesterday's Memories* remains a valuable reference tool for hard-core enthusiasts of rhythm and blues music between the late forties and early sixties. Its articles on musicians, producers, and other personalities involved with this genre are considered by some to be the most authoritative available in the periodical literature. The typical feature is appended by a discographical listing of recordings attributed to the individual (or group of individuals). The text often includes critical analyses of these recordings. Other noteworthy inclusions are book reviews of the important literary contributions to the rhythm and blues field and ads promoting the holdings of prominent nationwide dealers (the prices here can be utilized as a guideline to a fair price in the record-bargaining process).

Zigzag. Prestagate, Reading, England, 1971-. Monthly. Rate: $16.00 by sea, $27.00 by air/year (U.S. subscriptions); $1.50/issue.

A high-quality fanzine which attempts to seriously chronicle the contemporary music scenes of the United Kingdom and America. Both the articles and record reviews are expertly written. The duplication of much of its coverage in the less expensive mass-circulation periodicals of a generalist approach such as *Crawdaddy* and *Circus* renders *Zigzag* something of an unnecessary luxury. The print is very small; some individuals may require a magnifying glass to read it.

Chapter 4

AUDIO REPRODUCTION EQUIPMENT UTLIZED
IN A LIBRARY SETTING

INTRODUCTION

Most librarians will find it necessary to include sound recording equipment as part of their overall holdings. The amount
and type of equipment acquired will hinge upon the following
considerations:

1. The amount of space available within the library's
   physical plant
2. The size of the budgetary allotment in the area of
   sound recordings, i.e., the degree of priority accorded this sector relative to overall library spending.
3. The focal points with respect to record and tape
   holdings.
4. Staff and client needs

Many libraries are severely handicapped in the acquisition
of recorded sound hardware by a lack of available space. Those
institutions short either on space or equipment may find it
expedient to place their stress upon the circulation function.
Those libraries, however, which maintain predominantly reference collections will be required to provide adequate facilities

in the library for the monitoring of recordings. One distinct
advantage of reference collections is that the damage recordings incur through continued use is minimized. It is desire-
able to plan the layout of a music department in such a way as
to enable only trained staff to handle the recordings listened
to by patrons; this can be achieved by installing all phonographs and tape recorders behind staff desks. Patrons will
then be required to make their requests to the librarian at
some given outpost. No matter how short of space a library
may be, hardware will be vital to staff in carrying out various
functions such as (a) monitoring newly purchased records and
tapes for defects, (b) checking for damage to materials returned
by patrons, (c) weeding out inferior holdings, and (d) library services (e.g., reference, radio broadcasting, group presentations).

Budgetary considerations represent perhaps the most potentially limiting factor. A budget which enables a library
barely to provide adequate services in the print sector will
preclude the acquisition of significant amounts of audiovisual
hardware. However, the core of this problem often depends upon the priorities of staff members rather than funding limitations. Administrators may feel that devoting a considerable
fraction of the library budget to the sound recordings sector,
i.e., software as well as equipment, represents an unfeasible
objective. They may point to past user patterns or patron surveys to back up their decisions; the key here is in determining
whether or not such arguments have been objectively made.

A library which provides a significant protion of its budget for sound recordings is already half way towards realizing
this goal of adequate equipment holdings. An important consideration here will be to what extent the collection is committed
to either tape or record formats. For example, those archives
concerned primarily with the acquisition and reproduction of

field performances will be concerned more with the purchase
of tape recording and playback equipment rather than phonographs. Also, a community served by a public library which
generally can afford only an inexpensive phonograph or cassette player would be making an illogical choice by including
open-reel tapes for circulation.

For those institutions possessed of both the inclination
and demand on the part of their constituency to acquire equipment relating to the area of sound recordings, one way of
overcoming funding limitations would be to encourage gifts of
hardware which could not otherwise be afforded. Friends of
the library or direct requests to certain philanthropic groups
or individuals represent two possibilities with respect to
this approach.

The kinds of equipment most frequently utilized by libraries carrying sound recordings include the following:

1. Phonographs. The primary uses for these pieces of
   equipment are (a) client use in the library, (b) staff
   use in monitoring recordings, and (c) tape reproduction, radio broadcast Amplifiers, turntables, and
   speakers will be separate in the more expensive units.

2. Tape recorders. They are used for most of the same
   functions as phonographs. They consist of three major
   types, copen-reel, 8-track, and cassette. Some libraries may want to obtain a wire recorder in order
   to play old wire recordings. These recorders are no
   longer available for purchase from manufacturers.
   However, a skilled technician will have no trouble
   renovating and servicing an old one.

3. Optional equipment beyond the basic sound system such
   as equalizers and reverb units.

4. Radio broadcast equipment, which includes mixing
   boards, microphones, transmitters, and professional
   playback machinery.

5. Headphones for use in listening booths.

Figure 1 reveals the arrangement of such equipment within
the context of a floor plan for a music department.

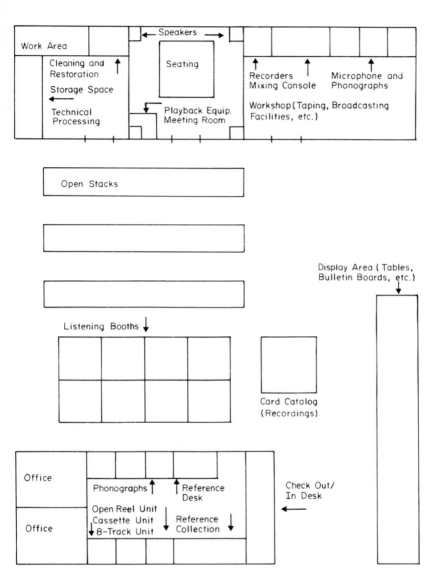

Chart reveals the arrangement of such equipment within the context of a floor plan for a music department.

6. Public-address speakers for use in large meeting rooms
    or auditoriums.

7. Selector panels, which enable patrons to decide the
    channel they want to use when listening to recordings
    in the library

8. Record and tape cleaning kits, including,
    a. Anti-static guns
    b. Vacuum systems
    c. Preener kits
    d. Chemical compounds (e.g., discwasher fluid)
    e. Dust-bug attachments
    f. Extras, such as cloths, brushes, and pads

THE BASIC SOUND SYSTEM

The purchase of audio reproduction equipment requires a knowl-

edge of the needs, capabilities, and financial limitations of

a given library.   Perhaps the main consideration in the pur-

chase of this equipment is that of monetary cost.   Some of the

questions which one might ask include,

How much money is available?

Is the purchase of a stopgap nature, or one which is en-
visioned as being long-term in its consequences?

If an entire audio system is being contemplated, would it
be best initially to get along without such luxury items
as tuners or channel selector boards in order to obtain
finer quality components for the rest of the system?

The heart of any sound system is a stereo phonograph.

This basic audio unit can be purchased as one piece of equip-

ment or in separate components consisting of speakers, ampli-

fier, and record changer.   Additional components such as tape

decks, tuners, and equalizers can be acquired as finances per-

mit.

The minimum investment for a stereo sound system possessed

of moderate-quality fidelity will be approximately $500 (tak-

ing into account retail discounts).   Spending increased amounts,

up to about $1500, will result in the realization of increased
dividends. Investments higher than $1500, however, will lead
up to the point of diminishing returns; a system costing
$1500-2000 can be acquired which provides a quality of sound
closely rivaling that of one valued at several times as much.

SPEAKERS

Speakers tend to fall into either of two main categories.
One type seeks to obtain a sonic absolute, possessing very
little sound of its own. Proponents of this type of speaker
want to hear only the information encoded in their program
sources, no matter how flawed it may be. For example, if a
recording is cut with little emphasis on the bass, these advocates would prefer to hear the music without bass as reproduced by an accurate system, rather than with the bass
jacked up through a speaker. Speakers aiming at sonic accuracy demand large expenditures and a good deal of care, for
they tend to be rather inefficient, necessitating large amounts
of amplifier power, and they frequently require exact place-
ment for the finest possible fidelity. Noteworthy low-priced
reproducers of this type include the lines of Advent, Fulton
Musical Industries, IMF, EPI, ESS, KLH,* Dynaco, and Acoustic
Research. The more expensive side of the ledger includes
Audio Research Magneplanars, Dahlquists, Infinity Servo-statik
"one-ays", and the Fulton-J modular speaker systems, which
range from $800 to $4000 per pair.

   The other type is comprised of ultra-efficient speakers
designed with the aim of providing a definite sound of their
own. This type can be characterized as having been endowed

*EPI (Epicure Products, Inc., Newburyport, Mass); Ess (ESS,
Inc, Sacramento, Calif.); KLH (KLH Research & Development
Corp., Cambridge, Mass.).

with boosted bass response, punchy midranges, and extrasharp
high ends so as to render the music more exciting. JBL,* Pioneer, and Altec represent a few of the companies providing
the hard, loud sound typified by ultraefficient speakers.

Proponents of this type of speaker note that it is
usually the class chosen to monitor and mix down commercial
recordings. Ultraefficient speakers are employed for this
task because the recording engineer requires a "loud" speaker
which sets forth all of the music's subtleties in no uncertain
terms. Advocates in this camp argue that since most recordings were produced by the ultraefficient system, they ought
to be played back via the same method.

Speaker prices are not necessarily indicative of the
units' merit for a particular listener. Speaker selection
is an extremely subjective process. Once a library's financial limits have been determined, the key to the purchase of
speakers is to listen to them beforehand; preferably with the
equipment one intends to use, and, if possible, within the
acoustic environment where they would ultimately be placed.
One should experiment at this time with various placements,
as the optimum sound for a given position will vary from
speaker to speaker.

It is recommended that librarians make sure that the
speaker cable measures at least 18-gauge; 12-gauge would be
preferable in cases where more than 25 feet of wire is used.
Skimping on the size of cable gauge can result in disastrous
consequences to the sound of a given speaker power, bass, and
clarity are lost if the cable used does not meet the demands
placed upon it.

Speakers represent only a fraction of the stereo component system. A good system requires that comparable amounts

---

*JBL (James B. Lansing Sound, Inc., Northridge, Calif.).

of attention paid to the selection of amplifiers and turntables, as has been recommended with respect to speakers.

AMPLIFIERS

The power amplifier comprises the heart of every audio system. A basic amp possessing few or no controls is teamed with a preamp (control unit) for volume, balance, tone controls, and mode selection to form the basic power unit. The amp and pre-amp can be acquired as separate units or built into one inte-grated amp. A receiver goes one step further in incorporating a radio tuner (AM and/or FM) into the unit. A receiver will not have the power of a basic amp of an identical price, while an integrated unit will fall somewhere in between the two. Use of a stereo system for background music, or within a small room, will render a receiver the logical choice. Serious listening, particularly with a larger room, will necessitate the use of at least 25-30 watts per channel as well as sepa-rate components. The component route is the most expensive, but allows much flexibility in upgrading the various parts of a system. It should also be noted that a compnent which only has to serve one function tends to do it better than the re-ceiver, which performs a multitude.

Excellent separate amps and preamps are marketed by Dynaco, Harman-Kardon, SAE,[*] Crown, Phase Linear, and Audio Research, among others. Marantz and Poneer are noteworthy for their in-tegrated amps, while Dynaco, Scott, Harman-Kardon, Kenwood, Marantz, Pioneer, and Sherwood all produce fine receivers.

When evaluating a receiver, one has to consider all of its performance facets, power, tuner selectivity and sensitiv-ity, control versatility, etc. As in the case of speakers, the best means of finding out which amplifier is most suitable

*SAE (Scientific Audio Electronics, Inc., Los Angeles, Calif.)

to the requirements of one's library is to try the various
models out in conjuction with the other components used in
that acoustic environment.

PHONO SYSTEMS

Again, going with separate compnents for the phono system represents the best albeit the most expensive approach in obtaining high-quality performance. A good setup comprising
tone arm, turntable, and cartridge, will retail at a minimum
of $200. A discount price of $100-$150 should be considered
the bare minimum; all units running less than $100 are little
more than children's gadgets. Some of the important ways in
which a phono unit should be evaluated are as follows:

Does the speed appear to be accurate?

Is there any noticeable degree of wow or flutter?

Does rumble provide a serious distraction?

Does the tone arm return to a cuing position after the
record has been played?

How many speeds can be selected? (The standard range is
33-1/3, 45, 78-rpm; some phonos include only 33-1/3 and
45. The inclusion of 16-2/3 rpm is a rarity.)

Does the turntable possess its own speed adjustment mechanism (in order to rectify errors which might develop by
hand)?

Does it have a 45 rpm changer which permits the stacking
of discs?

Does the dustcover lid close down while the record is being played?

Is the phono automatic or manual?

Does the turntable employ direct or belt drive?

Does the turntable possess an antiskate mechanism?

What is the quality of the parts used in the construction
of the unit?

What type of suspension is present? Is it located in the base or the turntable?

What type of cartridge makes recordings sound best or the most natural within a given library's acoustic environment?

Shure, Pickering, Empire, Stanton, and ADC[*] all produce fine cartridges within a variety of price ranges. While cartridges can be purchased that run as high as $500, little noticeable gain to the average listener will be obtained over the sonic quality provided by the Shure V15-III which carries a tag of less than $100. Stick with a cartridge that tracks under 2 grams. Do not set the tracking force at less than ½ gram; too little pressure can ruin many more discs than a bit too much. A cartridge which tracks at 1 gram or less should not be mated with an inexpensive changer or a heavily-weighted single-play arm. Look for trim, light tone arms, even if they appear to lack the durability of the heavier models.

An important point to remember is that, next to the quality of sound reproduced, the key function of a phono system is to protect one's records against unnecessary wear. A library can upgrade all of its components, except for a worn-out record collection.

OUTSIDE OF THE BASIC COMPONENT SYSTEM

Tape recorders represent perhaps the most challenging problem to librarians concerned with the selection of audio equipment. Those institutions possessed of a sufficiently large budget would do well to procure both a tape deck which plugs into a basic component system and a separate tape recorder in as many formats as possible. The self-contained unit, while lacking in general the acoustic excellence and diversity of functions

* ADC (Audio Dynamics Corp., Division at BSR Consumer Products Group, Blauvelt, New York).

characterizing a tape deck, possesses a greater degree of
flexibility with respect to where it is used. Taping equipment provides for the following functions:

1. Playback of recordings available only in this format
   or for some reason preferred in open-reel (e.g., extreme hiss in cassette or 8-track, poor surface
   quality of a given company's records).

2. Production of extra copies of a recording considered
   to be of value.

3. Savings in space by having records transferred to
   tape.

4. Providing one or more additional media for library
   users who may not possess record players.

5. Making it possible to produce lasting recordings of
   concerts, noteworthy speeches and debates, and other
   programs of merit.

A tape deck/recorder should be checked for the presence
(and performability) of these features:

1. Type of tape heads (e.g., glass, steel).

2. The presence of a third tape head to monitor a recording for errors or flaws while it is being made.

3. Does the recorder possess an overdub feature?

4. In the case of open-reel machines, can 10-inch reels
   be utilized?

5. Does the machine possess an automatic meter setting
   for use in the recording process?

6. Is a dustcover included?

7. Does the tape recorder possess a pause switch?

8. Is an automatic-reverse switch included for use in
   playback?

9. Does the machine have a built-in demagnetization
   unit?

10. Is an automatic timing device present?

11. How many different speeds are available (the standard
    options are 3-3/4 and 7-½ inches per second; some
    machines include 1-7/8 and 15 ips)?

12. Does the recorder possess a special "tape through" feature that enables one to copy tapes from one machine to another while listening to other program sources?

A good tape recorder or deck will cost at least $300. A great deal of the price tag for units retailing for more than $500 will be given over to extra features such as automactic reverse and an automatic meter setting for recording. Some librarians may feel that these accessories represent unnecessary frills in view of the added cost they entail. In such cases, it would be sensible for librarians to purchase machines which provide for only the most basic functions.

A much wider discrepancy exists between the prices of cassette decks and cassette players than is the case with decks and autonomous units in the open-reel sector. A good cassette deck costs at least $200. Cassette players are almost exclusively portable in nature and are considerably less expensive than a deck; a fine-quality player can be obtained for $75. What the cassette player gives away in sound quality, it more than makes up for with respect to maneuverability in use. Any library concerned with sound quality would do well to consider investing heavily in open-reel machinery. open-reel equipment provides greater possibilities by means of the features available as well as more control of the tape itself (e.g., editing, repairs). A cassette deck might well be preferable in cases where the cost of an open-reel machine is prohibitive.

An 8-track deck of good quality without the tape recording facet can be purchased for approximately $75. A deck which includes this capacity is comparable in cost to a cassette deck. The unwieldy aspects of 8-track cartridges (e.g., the constant interruptions for changes between channels) render cassette players a more practical alternative to the open-reel machine.

THE MATING OF COMPONENTS

The acquisition of first-rate individual components does not
assure that an audio product commensurate with the sum of
these parts will be achieved. Care should be taken in the
mating of various compnents in order to achieve the optimum
in sound quality. *Rolling Stone* magazine has provided its
own solution to the problem of mating components by listing
those sound systems presently on the market possessed of the
"brightest sound." (The latter phrase is not clearly defined
in the article, but would seem subject to some question as to
the type of sound which is implied, i.e., note the polariza-
tion between ultraefficiency and low efficiency, as discussed
earlier in the chapter.) This listing is as follows:

1. Under $500. Pioneer of American. Model KH-7766.
    Centrex System. Includes receiver, cassette unit,
    and BSR record changer (with magnetic cartride) all
    within one wood cabinet. Speakers are separate.

2. Around $600. Record player: BIC* 940 (Multiple Play),
    $120. Cartridge: Micro/Acoustics 2002e, $42.50, or
    Audio Technica At 12E, $55. Receiver: Sony STR-2800,
    $240, or Advent 300, $260. Speakers: EPI Model 100,
    $200/pair.

3. Under $1000. Record player: Philips GA-222, $230,
    or Garrard GT-55, $250. Cartridge: Pickering XV-15/
    625E, $60, or Shure M95ED, $65. Receiver: Kenwood
    KR-4600, $300. Speakers: New Advent, $300/pair; Avid
    103, $360/pair; or Koss CM-1010, $370/pair.

4. Around $1500. Record player: Dual 1245, $230, or
    JVC JL-F50, $250. Cartridge: Staton 681EEE, $90, or
    Shure V15-III, $85. Receiver: Hitachi SR-903, $99.95
    Speakers: Allison II, $600/pair; Dahlquist DQ-10,
    $790/pair; or Technics SB-7000A, $800/pair.

5. Under $2000. Record player: BIC 1000, $290; Technics
    by Panasonic or Pickering XSV-3000, $100. Receiver:
    JVC JR-600 (MK II), $600, or Lux 1050, $595. Speakers
    Infinity Quantum 5, $640/pair; Rectilinear 7a, $900/

---

*BIC (British Industries Co.); Westbury, New York

pair; or Quad ESL, $930/pair.

6. Around $2000. ADC (BSR) Accutrac +6, $400, or Pioneer PLC-590, Receiver: Yamaha CR-2020, $700, or Pioneer SX-1250, $900. Speakers: Audioanalyst M-8 $700/pair, or Bose 901-III, $767/pair.

7. Around $3500. Record Player: ADC (BSR) Accutrac 4000, $600, or $100. Receiver: Tandberg 2075, $1099, or Sansue TU-9900 tuner, $460, plus either Sherwood HP-2000 integrated amplifier, $750, or Kenwood 600 integrated amplifier, $750. Speakers: Acoustic Research (AR) 10 "pi," $800/pair, or JBL L300, $1920/pair.

8. Around $5000. Record player: Bang & Olufsen 4002, $740 (includes cartridge MMC-4000). Tuner: Nakamichi 630 tuner-preamp, $630, plus Nakamichi 620 power amplifier, $630; or Yamaha CT-7000 tuner, $1200, plus Sansue BA-2000 (depending on finish)/pair, or Bozak B-410, $2500/pair.

9. Under $6000. Record player: Technics by Panasonic SP-10 Mk II, $700, or Lux PD-121, $500, either with Shure SME 3009 tone arm, $174. Cartridge: Audio Technica AT15Sa, $100. Tuner: Sherwood Micro/CPU 100, $2000, plus Soundcraftsmen PE2217 preamp, $530, plus McIntosh MC-2205 power amplifier, $1200. Speakers: JBL L212, $1750.

10. Around $12,000. Record player: JVC QL-10, $1200. Cartridge: Audio C-1 preamp, $1800, plus Stax (American Audioport) DA-300 power amplifier, $3600. Speakers: Altec Model 19, $1318/pair, or Dayton-Wright XG-8 Mk 3, $2940/pair.

Rolling Stone has also listed four cassette and open-reel decks, respectively, felt to be "representative of the best the industry has to offer at various price levels."[2]

Cassette decks:

Kenwood KX-920. Under $300.

JVC Model KD-75. Under $380.

Nakamichi 600. Around $550.

Tendberg TCD-330. Under $1000.

Open-reel Machines:

Teac A-6100. Around $1000.

Technics by Panasonic. RS-1500US. Around $1500.

Pioneer RT-2044. Around $1600.

Revox A-700. Around $1800.

There used to be a noticeable degree of difference between studio tape machines employed by professionals and
home equipment with respect to (a) standing up to continuous
use, and (b) the presence of built-in features providing for
a variety of additional functions. However, in recent years,
home tape decks have come close to matching the level of
performance provided by professional equipment.

OPTIONAL EQUIPMENT

The following accessories might be considered by libraries as
worthy of inclusion among their array of audio hardware.
Much of this equipment years, but has only recently been
marketed for homes and institutions outside the music industry
mainstream.

1. Headphones.

2. Reverberation amplifiers, which can produce an assort-
    ment of special effects via distortion. While the
    most vocal opposition to these units will come from
    audio purists favoring a natural sound, the major
    danger lies in the potential havoc which the large
    amounts of feedback generated by reverberators can
    wreak upon amplifier circuitry. Those libraries
    possessing expensive equipment would do well to avoid
    usage of reverb units.

3. Frequency equalizers, which complement amplifiers by
    boosting all ranges of the audio spectrum.. Such
    an accessory should not be necessary with the more
    expensive amplifiers currently available.

4. The Dolby noise-reduction system, which functions
    primarily to filter out undesirable hiss in open-
    reel and cassette machines without strongly inter-
    fering with the recorded sound output.

5. Pop-and-click eliminators. Actually a variation of the Dolby concept, this device is concerned with filtering out noises on discs caused by either manufacturing flaws or poor care on the part of the user.

6. Expanders and companders. The former restores the full dynamic range characteristic of a live performance; in the past this was available only on master tapes to the compressed renditions emanating from radio, discs, commercial tapes, etc. Companders enable the user to first compress live recorded sound on to tape and then expand then to their original dynamic range during playback. This process also provides some degree of noise reduction.

7. Audio time-delay units, which function to "enlarge" one's acoustic environment in order that it take on the dimensions of any setting from a steamy little pub to a large concert hall. The equipment entails a small amp and two speakers.

For ratings of the various types of audio components see Appendix 2 at the end of the text.

NOTES

1. "Choice Pickings," *Rolling Stone*, September 8, 1977, p. 51.

2. *Ibid.*, pp. 103-104.

Chapter 5

THE CARE AND PRESERVATION OF
SOUND RECORDINGS

INTRODUCTION

The care and preservation of sound recordings is a process
which must begin from the moment the materials arrive at the
library; it enbraces the technical processing, storage, and
use of discs and tapes.

The role of personnel in the technical processing department consists of (a) checking to see if the correct discs and
tapes have been received and whether or not they are in good
condition, and (b) exercising sufficient care in preparing
them for the shelves so as to avoid damage before actual use.
It is imperative that librarians not hesitate to return recordings which are in poor condition upon reception.

There are five major types of disc storage: horizontal,
off-vertical stacking, spring-loaded vertical stacking, full-
compartment vertical stacking, and template-controlled vertical
stacking. The first three storage types result in surface
imprinting while horizontal and off-vertical stacking cause
warpage; therefore, the latter two types rate best with respect
to quality of record care. However, with the advent of browser
boxes, which employ off-vertical stacking, a conflict has

arisen between concerns of public taste and the best possible record care. Tape storage variations are not much of a factor in that the boxes and reels on which tapes are wound protect them from physical damage.

Perhaps the key issue with respect to the storage issue is the conflict between adherents for open access and those opposed to it. The basic arguments of each camp are provided in Table 2.

Records and tapes both require moderate temperatures (between 55 and 70°F with low humidity and adequate ventilation). The storage area should also be kept well-dusted so as to avoid unnecessary deterioration.

A major issue relevant to the use of sound recordings concerns their handling by both patrons and library staff. Personnel often set bad examples by their own poor record and tape handling techniques for the public. Such a problem can be rectified by training staff properly before they begin working in the sound recordings sector. It is also important that library playback equipment be of sufficiently high quality and proper working order so as to ensure the continued life of the recording.

It is much more difficult to monitor the treatment which discs and tapes receive when circulated outside of the library. Unless a librarian can closely observe a patron's actual handling techniques, he will be forced to act in good faith. One means of helping to control this problem would be to provide handouts to patrons which outline proper handling methods. Another approach would be to explain certain techniques in person. A great deal of tact is necessary in order to achieve the desired results in the latter case. The ultimate determinant as to a user's desirability with respect to checking out recordings will come upon an inspection of the returned materials. While the library runs the risk of having an arm

TABLE 2: Pros and Cons of Open Access to Recordings

For open access	Against open access
1. Closed access is outdated for books and is already out-dated for records and tapes.	1. Recordings are not books, and arguments based on book techniques are ir-relevant.
2. Open access saves space and is therefore an advantage when space is short.	2. Fewer records and sleeves can be accommodate in brow-ser boxes than in sleeves only. The records them-selves, can often be fitted into space which would not be suitable for public access.
3. Problems arise in connection with the storage of records in browser boxes, as the discs are not as well-sup-ported as on proper record shelving. However, in busy libraries records are out on loan more often than not, and in any case the advantages of complete open access out-weigh the disadvantages of less satisfactory storage.	3. Browser boxes not not suit-able for storing LP's for long periods. Busy librar-ies may have few records in the boxes at any time but those with less demand may have a large proportion of their records stored in this way.
4. Records and sleeves are all in one place. The public does not have to collect re-cords from another part of the library.	4. Records stored in browser boxes must be protected from sunshine, radiators, etc., but record sleeves only can be placed in any well-lit and heated part of the library and will not suffer.
5. Theft and damage through handling of records is low.	5. Theft is a problem with open access; however, there is little point in stealing sleeves only.

load of recordings returned in unusable condition, at least damages by the particular user can be avoided in the future. There are a number of things to look for when inspecting for damage:

1. An inspection of the record surface for obvious scratches, cracks, chips, warpage, or excessive wear. Staff must learn to distinguish between superficial scratches and deep scratches which reach into the bottom portions of the groove, where the needle tracks. Superficial scratches and nicks will not affect the sound quality or the discs fidelity, whereas the deep ones will cause annoying pops and ticks which seriously impede listener enjoyment. Those discs where the librarian suspects that serious damage has occurred should be played on staff equipment so as to ascertain the full extent of the damage The action taken with the patron will depend entirely on a given library's policy in such matters; however, accurate and up-to-date records of a disc's condition should be kept. These records be jotted down in the upper portion of the circulating card kept in library files when the disc is checked out. By this means, a patron will not be blamed for damage for which he is not responsible. In order to pinpoint the exact location of damage, the librarian might divide each side of the recording into four imaginary quarters and label the section in which the damage has occurred.

2. Tapes should be run through a machine at reverse (if the tape was not rewound by the patron) or at both fast forward and reverse. This procedure will enable the librarian to determine whether or not the tape has been broken. Warpage can be detected by the naked eye. Unfortunately one cannot ascertain the more subtle types of damage such as accidental erasure or sound distortion unless the entire tape is run through at the regular playback speed. This is highly impractical for the librarian in that it would consume far too much time.

While it is desirable that some degree of control be exercised in the circulation of sound recordings, librarians must be careful not to give an impression to their clientele of being too restrictive. Criticism of a patron's treatment of recordings should be dealt tactfully.

Equally important, however, is the need for staff to formulate a policy as to exactly what constitutes adequate treatment of records and tapes. Consistency must be maintained in the interpretation of such a policy.

THE CLEANING OF PHONOGRAPH RECORDINGS

The cleaning of records can greatly prolong their life span;
this should be done both before the disc is made available for
public use and at regular intervals afterwards. The fact that
today's high-fidelity systems possess a degree of excellence
far surpassing the technical development of most vinyl pressings
renders it all the more imperative that records be continually
maintained in the best possible condition. The records of the
present day remain, as did their predecessors, highly vulnerable
to dust and other types of debris, as well as static electricity.
Fortunately, a wide variety of cleaners have appeared on the
market in the past decade which can be of invaluable assistance
in preserving the condition of phonograph records. Perhaps
the first step in the move toward better record care is the
acquisition of a high-powered, and preferably flexible, lamp
which enables accurate appraisal of disc surfaces. It is vital
to know just what the condition of a record is in order to
ensure that it is cleaned properly and efficiently.

While it is universally recognized that embedded dirt
particles can undermine the quality of sound reproduced from a
disc surface, the buildup of electrostatic charges represents
a less widely appreciated form of erosion which can be equally
devastating to the life of a record. The following devices
have been commercially produced which help to reduce electrostatic charges:

1. The Watts Preener Kit employs a nylon roller with an
   internal core impregnated with an ionic compound.
   The compound combats static build-up when the nylon
   roller is pushed in the circular direction of the record's grooves.

2. The Megafilare brush marketed by AEC utilizes miniscule
   consuctive nylon bristles to reduce static charges;
   it dispenses with the need for fluids or compounds.

3. The Staticmaster 500 (Nuclear Products), with a re-
    tractable 3-inch-wide brush and a slightly radioactive
    polonium element, attracts smaller dust particles as
    well as combatting static.

4. The Zerostat produces antistatic high voltage when a
    "trigger" is activated.

The removal of dust and other debris can be achieved by a
number of time-proven methods:

1. Vacuuming, as with the Vac-O-Rec system.

2. The chemical approach. A leader in this field for
    some time has been Discwasher; it markets a special
    fluid which, when applied to an accompanying brush
    containing slanted unidirectional fibers, effectively
    removes dust and other debris, and functions as an
    antistatic guard. The primary advantage of the chemi-
    cal school is that it enables the removal of microdust
    (e.g., fingerprints) not cleared away by preeners or
    vacuum devices. The best chemical compounds are based
    upon a formula which cleans thoroughly but is suffici-
    ently gentle so as to leave delicate vinyl polymers
    flexible and strong. The Discwasher fluid can also be
    applied to a Watts Dust-Bug or similar device with
    great effectiveness in combatting the build-up of statis
    and debris. The Dust-Bug, as well as Audio Technica's
    AT-6002 and the Bibs Groove Kleen Tone Arm, consists
    of a miniature tone arm with a brush-roller combination
    mounted at one end. The other end is secured by a
    clamp or suction device next to the turntable at the
    base of the phonograph.

3. Washing. This method is probably the most controver-
    sial of all with respect to the benefits derived from
    its application. Use of the wrong compounds can result
    in causing more damage to a record than previously ex-
    isted. However, in some cases, washing a disc may re-
    present the only successful means of cleaning it. One
    approach which has proven effective is the use of a
    mild dishwater detergent: 2 drops to 2 quarts of water
    should be mixed in a shallow basin. Distilled water
    is preferable to the tap variety in that it contains
    none of the impurities present in drinking water. These
    impurities may settle in the grooves of a disc after
    the water has evaporated, thereby resulting in further
    erosion of the sound quality during playback. A nylon
    brush with fine bristles should be employed in the
    washing of records. Watts has manufactured a brush

expressly for this purpose. Washing should be done
in the direction of the record grooves rather than
across them. The surface should then be rinsed with
water. Drying is accomplished best by utilizing a
two-step process: (a) first, lightly rubbing the
disc surface (again, in the direction of the grooves)
with a clean cotton cloth, and (b) then utilizing a
preener or brush to soak up the remaining moisture
which has settled in the grooves.

4.   A more sophisticated approach to cleaning records is
the "wet-play" system. A typical example, the
Lenoclean system, is comprised of an arm with a hollow
tube-shaped reservoir. The fluid contained within
this storage space consists primarily of ethyl alcohol
and distilled water. A plastic brush with a head for
controlling the amount of fluid released is the heart
of this system. It ensures that the stylus rides in
a bath of rapidly drying fluid. The wet-play approach
has been documented to prevent excess wear by greatly
reducing heat and friction at the point of contact
between stylus and disc.

Dry lubricants provide protection against record wear comparable to that achieved by the wet-play system. They possess
the added advantage of reducing the danger of clogged grooves
which exists with the wet-play approach. Records previously
treated with antistatic sprays, cloths, or brushes will leave
a mixture of chemicals and debris in the grooves, which, in
turn results in the formation deposits that stick to the groove
walls when the wet-play technique is employed. In order to
avoid this problem, those individuals wishing to utilize the
wet-play system must first wash their discs. However, washing
is not necessary when using the dry lubricants. To be sure, a
disc has to be clean before applying the lubricant so as to
prevent the bonding of contaminants already on its surface.
But the use of chemical cleaners such as the brush and fluid
marketed by Discwasher is sufficient in preparing the record
for treatment with the dry lubricant.

One of the leading dry lubricants presently on the market
is Sound Guard. Applied in spray form, Sound Guard is then
buffed in for several minutes on each side of the record. It
provides a thin dry layer that functions both as a lubricant
and a shield against disc wear. In order to ensure optimum
sound protection, records treated in this manner should continue
to be cleaned on a regular basis. Discwasher also puts out a
dry lubricant, called the Pro-Disc Environment, which is less
time-consuming to use than the Sound Guard kit.

A dirty stylus can be as destructive to records as electrostatic charges and debris which remain unattended to. The
Watts Nylon Stylus Cleaner and Discwasher's SC-I, featuring a
retractable brush and magnifying mirror so as to inspect the
stylus, represent two of the most frequently used stylus
cleaners. A camel's-hair brush will often be sufficient for
cleaning styli devoid of particularly heavy build-ups of foreign material. An important rule of thumb here is to avoid
touching the stylus with one's hands. This practice is rather
widespread among uninformed hi-fi enthusiasts as a means of
dislodging dust and other types of debris from the stylus.
Not only does such a practice often lead to permanently damag-
ing the stylus (eg., chipping the needle, bending the base of
the stylus), but it results in the presence of an oily residue
which is in turn transferred from the needle to the disc.

Several other tips should be observed in order to avoid
undermining the positive results ensuing out of the application
of the above techniques:

1. Do not leave a disc open to the environment for ex-
    tended periods of time. When a record is not in use
    return it immediately to its sleeve. If at all pos-
    sible, employ a dustcover while a disc is being played.

2. Keep the phonograph--particularly those components
    which come into direct contact with the record (e.g.,
    the turntable platter and tone arm) free of dust and

other debris at all times. The natural propensity of
records to retain a static charge will render the
transfer of such dirt to a disc rotating on the platter
almost inevitable.

3. Avoid sneezing, coughing, or smoking when near an ex-
    posed disc, as the impurities sent out into the at-
    mosphere may find their way on to the record surface.
    Even talking can be detrimental to the optimum care
    of records.

THE CLEANING OF RECORDING TAPE

The cleaning of tapes is considerably harder than the cleaning
of discs due to the length and inaccessibility of their playing
surface. Access to the surface of recording tape involves the
unraveling of hundreds (or thousands) of feet of material.
And, although tape may not appear to be as susceptible to
erosion by means of electrostatic charges, dirt, and other
debris, the results will ultimately be equally as devastating.

     Due to the problems presented in the cleaning of tapes,
the best approach to their care is one of prevention. This
can be achieved by following two important rules:

1. Keep the machinery for playing and reproducing tapes
    in clean working order. Each of the three main tape
    formats possesses its own type of equipment; however,
    each of these types of machinery requires basically
    a similar means of upkeep. It is of utmost import-
    ance that the tape heads on all of these machines be
    cleaned periodically with a solvent. Most retail out-
    lets concerned with recorded sound market some kind
    of head cleaner. But denatured alcohol will function
    just as efficiently in removing the grime and deposits
    from the tape surface which tend to build up on the
    heads with continued use. Application is best ac-
    complished with a cotton swab; it is vital that no
    material be used which will leave residue on the head
    (e.g., paper tissue). Equally necessary is the per-
    iodic demagnetization of the heads so as to prevent

the build-up of electrostatic charges which can event-
ually cause a recording to deteriorate in quality.
An excellent demagnetizer can be purchased for under
$10. The demagnetizer should be placed about ½-inch
away in a straight, steady movement. The demagnetizer
should also be kept as far away as is possible from
recorded tapes when it is plugged in and in use. If
this rule is not observed, the tapes in question will
possibly be damaged as a result of outer disturbance
to their magnetic particles. These particles supply
the code material which make the initial recording
possible. Also, one must see to it that all portions
of the tape player, are kept clean, particularly those
movable parts which come into direct contact with the
tape. Alcohol may be used on the metal parts but
should not be applied to rubber and plastic materials.
A soft, dry cloth ought to be sufficient in most cases
for these parts.

2. Keep all tapes stored in an environment protected from
outside contaminants. The best means of accomplishing
this is, as in the case of the disc, to keep tapes in
their storage boxes when not in use. If possible,
keep the tape covered while in use; this is usually
achieved by means of the compartments constructed in
8-track and cassette players for housing the cartridge
when being played. Open-reel tapes present more of a
problem because they tend to play for much longer periods of time and are rarely played on machines which
possess a device which can cover the reels while in
use.

Although it cannot be accomplished with an ease comparable
to discs, the cleaning of tapes is possible if the circumstances
require it. Open-reel tapes can be cleaned by lightly pinching
the tape from both sides with a soft cloth (preferably one
treated with a gently solvent such as Discwasher) while the
machine is set on "rewind." Cassette and 8-track cartridges
cannot be cleaned easily in this manner unless one opens up
the plastic casing in which the tape rests. These cartridges,
however, are tolerant of some degree of dirt build-up; the
important concern is to keep the hardware in clean working order.

NOTES

1. John W. Howes. "The storage and issue of sound recordings," in *Phonograph Record Libraries: Their Organization and Practice* (Henry F.J. Currall, ed.), 2d ed., Archon, Hamden, Conn., 1970, p. 85.

Chapter 6

ARRANGEMENT AND CLASSIFICATION
OF SOUND RECORDINGS

CENTRALIZATION VERSUS DEPARTMENTALIZATION

The controversy between the proponents of centralization and
those of departmentalization has not been resolved, to the
present day. The arguments of both camps reveal some merit
and will be outlined briefly here. The advantages of centralization include the following:

1. Greater efficiency in the arrangement, cataloging,
    and acquisition functions. When each of these func-
    tions is focused on one area, the possibility that
    they will be accomplished with greater speed and ac-
    curacy is enhanced considerably. Some libraries
    possess a combination of centralization and depart-
    mentalization with respect to these functions. For
    example, the music department of a library may do all
    of the ordering of discs and tapes for the other sec-
    tors, even though they each house their own record-
    ings. Such an arrangement may result in increased
    efficiency; however, this gain could be at the ex-
    pense of the knowledgeable selection provided by
    members of each department within their respective
    areas of specialization.

2. It enables the presence of a staff specifically trained
    in audiovisual methods.

3. It enables the achievement of more widespread use of
    the equipment necessary to utilize recorded sound re-
    sources.

4. It allows a greater visual impact upon the public
    which, presumably, results in increased use of the
    record collection.

The advantages of departmentalization include:

1. Maintaining the integrity of subject departmentali-
    zation with respect to library resources in general.

2. The staff possesses a closer working knowledge of the
    recorded sound collection.

3. It represents a means by which to attract new users;
    that is, people looking for print materials in a
    given subject area, could be given sound recordings
    instead by library personnel.

The route chosen by a given library will depend upon its particular set of circumstances. With the increasing growth of
the amounts of sound recordings in library collections, departmentalization has generally represented the course of
action chosen by all but the smallest institutions.

ARRANGEMENT AS A FACTOR IN THE MERCHANDIZING
OF RECORDED SOUND COLLECTIONS

Ideally, the arrangement of sound recordings should function as
more than a pathfinder for the location of selections which
a patron has decided upon, following a perusal of the card
catalog. It should provide a strong stimulus to browsers to
listen to recordings in the library and/or check them out in
much the same way that various displays in a record store are
meant to encourage the customer to purchase more discs and tapes
than he had originally intended. The rationale for this type
of aggressive merchandizing is that it enables libraries to
thrust themselves into the forefront of contemporary service
institutions while carrying none of the negative implications

of the hard sell which erodes the pocketbook of the consumer.

Libraries can learn a great deal from retail store techniques in the arrangement of sound recordings. Record album
jackets frequently feature eye-catching designs and illustrations. It is in the best interest of the library to exploit
this innate visual appeal in such a way as to promote optimum
use of the sound recordings collection. The use of browser
boxes represents a way of allowing patrons immediate access to
records with a minimum amount of effort. Wooden or wire racks
for records or tapes provide another viable alternative. It
is unlikely, however, that either browser boxes or racks would
be desirable for housing a complete collection unless the
holdings are inconsequential in nature. Another problem with
the use of these types of arrangement is that the records are
subject to a greater degree of warpage than when stored snugly
back-to-back in an upright position.

Special displays located at strategic outposts within the
library (sometimes completely outside the music department)
can also stimulate an interest in sound recordings. Such displays are usually set up on tables, cabinets, or bulletin boards.
It is a good idea to store the records somewhere else when the
jackets are being employed in such a manner. Exhibits of sound
recordings can focus upon a wide variety of themes, including
"new acquisitions," works of a well-known artist, or even the
presence of soical protest in music. A staff well-versed in
current events can capitalize upon this knowledge in its displays as a means of generating client interest. For instance,
news that a certain performer is coming to the area to give a
concert will be in itself a strong stimulus to increased interest in hearing his recordings. Librarians can enhance this
interest, while channeling some of it into the use of library
materials and services, by means of publicizing the availability
of library recordings by this particular artist.

The means by which the collection is divided up is as important as displays and convenient access in the encouragement
of sound recordings use in libraries. The use of a system
which has little relationship to the conceptual framework of
partrons will be detrimental to optimum use of the collection.
An example of such a system would be the ordering of the shelves by means of record company serial numbers, a scheme which
bears no similarity to the listening tastes of any particular
audience, No one would want to browse through a collection
which locates the sort of recordings desired at points widely
dispersed from each other. A far more practical arrangement
would consist of an alphabetical scheme by, say, composer and/
or performer, within a comparatively small number of broad subject headings. The application of this type of collection-
structuring system will enable the user to navigate in a manner
to which he is familiar in addition to allowing him to have all
of the recordings in his preferred genre in one general area.
Retail stores have utilized the broad subject/alphabetical
categorization approach for some time.

GENERAL CATALOGING PRINCIPLES

A number of theories of cataloging exist which are being applied
in some form or another at this time. The major ones are the
legalistic, the perfectionistic, the bibliographic, and the
pragmatic[1]. The former three entail a proliferation of cataloging rules as well as descriptive information on the cards.
In contrast with the above theories, the pragmatic approach
considers rules and other terminology important only insofar
as they maintain the integrity of the catalog on an everyday
working basis. In other words, legalistic verbiage and bibliographic details are not allowed to exist as ends in themselves.
The impulse to privde a catalog card which will satisfy all

users and provides explanations for every imaginable question that presents itself would appear to rest completely within the province of librarians' needs, rather than arising out of a recognition of the means by which to best assist their clientele.

Some institutions, most notably university and research libraries, may find it of value to include an exhaustive compilation of rules and obscure descriptive notes such as "Head and tail pieces," "Title vignette," and "Illustrated lining-papers" as part of their cataloging procedure. There would certainly seem to be little doubt that an institution which counts as its major focus the preservation and study of rare books would be concerned with documenting such minor bibliographic details in the catalog. Within the realm of sound recordings, an archive centered around historical jazz discs will operate under many of the same preconditions as a collection primarily concerned with rare books.

The legalisitic approach aims at formulating rules for every conceivable situation; most libraries, however, will find this approach undesirable for the following reasons:

1. It attempts to impose steadfast definitions in those cases where a solution would be better left indefinite. An example of this is the Anglo-American cataloging code which has sought to arbitrarily dictate the choice of entry with respect to both print and audiovisual materials. In some circles it is felt that questions requiring personal judgment are too intangible to adapt satisfactorily to the confining rules which characterize cataloging.

2. The cataloger remains entrapped by a process which demands a solution to all conceivable problems. When a problem crops up for which no rule has been formulated, the cataloger is required to amend the existing corpus of principles with a new ruling.

3. Preoccupation with the legalistic approach tends to undermine an understanding of the purpose of cataloging. The time and energy expended in the continual promulgation of new rules will detract immeasurably from the practical value of cataloging, which is to

provide an efficient means of identifying one's information needs and then to enable the user to locate
the source containing that information.

In recognition of the freedom it provides librarians in
constructing a catalog based upon user needs, the pragmatic
approach would seem to represent the best alternative for the
majority of institutions possessing collections of sound recordings.

TOWARD STANDARDIZATION IN THE CATALOGING OF
SOUND RECORDINGS

Despite long-ranging arguments within the field of librarianship as to whether a library should even include sound recordings in its collection, librarians have generally come to realize that this medium represented an indispensible means of
preserving and utilizing information. Nevertheless, the cataloging of discs and tapes remains stunted by the lack of
standardization. According to Jay Daily, the following situation has arisen out of this scarcity of standardization:

> each library tends to develop its own rules if it
> does not use Library of Congress cards. These have
> been found rather less than adequate for most li-
> raries because of the difficulty of locating the
> card for a phonorecording, the delays in cataloging,
> and the limitation to phonorecordings that the Li-
> brary of Congress acquires. The situation has be-
> come further confused by the necessity for libraries
> to catalog whatever is locally made. With the im-
> provement in techniques of recording and of re-
> producing sound has come the increased possibility
> that every library or institution can be its own
> producer of phonorecordings, for which no cataloging
> service outside the library is ever available....
> Although the library of Congress follows the Anglo-
> American Cataloging Rules of 1967, these were the
> subject of criticism soon after they were published,
> and most music libraries find them woefully inadequate[2].

Perhaps the major problems characterizing the cataloging
of sound recordings are (a) the presence of descriptive information which differs considerably from that of print material,
and (b) the necessity of far more entries than in the case of
books and serials. Descriptive information such as song programming (as well as composers for these individual tunes),
record/tape speed, type of format, color of vinyl, print inclusions, etc., should all be noted on a catalog card when
possible. With respect to the latter problem, a couple of examples should suffice. For instance, Fathers and Sons (Chess),
a recording considered to be classic joining of black blues and
white rock artists, would require the following entries:

1. Title.
2. Performers: Otis Spann, Michael Bloomfield, Paul
   Butterfield, Donald "Duck" Dunn, Dam Lay, etc.
3. Producer: Norman Dayron.
4. Compsers: McKinley Morganfield, Willie Dixon, etc.
5. Super Cosmic Joy-Scout Jamboree, the live concert which
   comprises sides three and four of this double-album set.

Alternatively, an opera would necessitate entries for the title
of the work, composer, librettist, conductor, the principal
vocalists, and the opera company.

Up until the present time, cataloging of sound recordings
has varied from the inclusion of maximum information to little
more than a main entry listing. The key here is one of determining (a) the number of entries, and (b) the amount of information needed in a given library so as to enable access to a
recording with relative ease on the part of the patron while
requiring minimal effort on the part of the cataloger.

While the amount of cataloging to be done by a given library will vary according to considerations such as staff time
available, the character of the clientele, and the type of recording, an excellent method applicable to all situations has

been set forth by Daily[3]. This system entails ten basic fields of description, most of which can be utilized as facets of access via the unit-entry format if necessary. These fields are:

1. Title (the principal entry).
2. Composer, librettist, etc.
3. Performers.
4. Producer, distributor.
5. Identifying number.
6. Physical description (e.g., size and speed of discs)
7. Distributor's serial number.
8. Additional description (used for identifying features that are not meant to be employed as access entries, such as arrangers of music, lyricists, the original work from which the item was derived, etc.).
9. Contents.
10. Subject headings.

The practical application of these fields of description to the cataloging of a sound recording is provided below.

FIELD	DESCRIPTION
1	<u>Tommy</u>.
2	Pete Townshend, with contributions by John Entwistle, Keith Moon, and Sonny Boy Williamson.
3	The Who.
4.	Decca.
5	DXSW 7205.
6	2 12-inch LPs; Stereo.
7.	(Omit)
8	Kit Lambert.
9	<u>Side one</u>: Overture; It's A Boy; You Didn't Hear It; Amazing Journey; Sparks; Eyesight to the Blind. <u>Side Two</u>: Christmas; Cousin Kevin; The Acid Queen; Underture. Side three: Do You Think It's Alright; Fiddle About; Pinball Wizard; There's A

Doctor I've Found; Go to the Mirror Boy;
Tommy Can You Hear Me; Smash the Mirror;
Sensation.

10   Music, Popular (Songs, etc.)--Great Britain.

The advantage of such a system is that it provides a
standardized pattern of identifying elements for a given recording which librarians (i.e., catalogers) can then rank ac-
ording to their value in providing subject access and identification. The fields of description can easily be adapted to
use by computer for purposes of producing the catalog. According to Daily, the first part of the entry

> should be the field that will eliminate confusion
> and provide least duplication. It is not necessarily
> the same for all the different kinds of phonorecords.
> Serious music can very well be entered under the
> composer with the unit entry always beginning with
> a composer's name. This is obviously unnecessary
> if the computer will be used to provide lists of
> phonorecordings arranged by whatever field is
> desired. A card catalog, however, is another
> proposition altogether. If only serious music is
> included, then arranging the unit entry so that
> the composer field, Field Two, is the entry line
> will eliminate duplication in the tracing and at
> least one card. As the number and kind of phono-
> recordings increase, especially if several different
> performances of a single work are available, this
> becomes an unreliable method of saving cards and
> space, because whatever is gained by the style of
> entry may be lost as the user requires help in
> order to search the card catalog for the information
> he needs.[4]

Since 1958, the Library of Congree has been providing pre-
printed cards for those libraries that have found them worth
the cost which they entail. Some of the disadvantages of employing these cards are as follows:

1. They will not cover locally prepared sound recordings
    and those manufactured abroad; that is, the printed
    cards produced by the Library of Congress are generally

limited to discs and tapes obtained from commercial
concerns and produced in this country.

2. Their use renders it almost imperative that Library of
    Congress subject headings already be a part of the
    library's existing scheme. For example, a library
    employing the Sears list will require a great deal of
    revision before the cards are usable.

3. The Library of Congress cataloging scheme places little
    emphasis upon the performer in sound recordings; that
    is, it represents a main entry system placing the
    primary attention upon either the composer or the
    title. In a library carrying many recordings in which
    the performer is of prime importance (popular music),
    the Library of Congress cards will not adequately do
    the job required of them.

4. Library of Congress cards may be hard for certain
    patrons to understand. This problem is complicated
    by locally prepared cards not conforming to the methods
    utilized by the Library of Congress. In other words,
    for locally produced and foreign recordings, there
    exists the possibility that inaccuracies will appear
    as a result of some misunderstanding by the cataloger
    of the Library of Congress scheme or mere errors of a
    clerical nature.

5. Delays in the ordering and receipt of Library of Con-
    gress cards may cause unnecessary hardships for both
    the library and its clientele.

On the other hand, use of Library of Congress cards can
lead to savings of both time and money. The primary preconditions in order that these savings be realized are as follows:

1. The collection should be relatively small.

2. It should be limited to recordings obtained from com-
    mercial sources and produced in the United States.

3. The library in question should already be employing
    library of Congress subject headings and preferably
    the Library of Congress cards themselves.

4. The need to catalog recordings should not be necessary
    within a comparatively short time span.[5]

The void which will be caused by the Library of Congress' decision to discontinue its service of issuing printed cards will
be filled by commercial companies such as Bro-Dart in the future.

As noted previously, personal cataloging represents another viable alternative to use of the Anglo-American system.
Its advantages would include the following:

1. Depending upon the system employed, it could be more
    efficient in terms of time and cost factors.

2. It should be easier for patrons and staff alike to
    understand.

3. It enables the application of more imaginative ideas
    in attempting to arrive at a solution to cataloging
    problems.

4. The time lag between the reception of discs and tapes
    cataloging will be cut down considerably.

5. It permits the flexible utilization of main entries
    which best reflect the types of recordings in the
    collection. An example of the shortcomings of the
    Anglo-American rules is that they pay little attention
    to the performer.

However, some librarians may feel that the disadvantages
inherent in the application of the personal touch in cataloging
outweigh the advantages.   These disadvantages include:

1, It encourages a greater number of errors (both of a
    clerical and judgmental nature.)

2. It may be hard to maintain a feasible degree of con-
    sistency with respect to the application of cataloging
    maxims in utilizing a personalized approach.

3. The application of this approach may result in a lack
    of standardization in dealings between libraries.
    Functions such as cataloging, acquisitions, and lend-
    ing on an interlibrary basis of cooperation can be
    undermined to a great extent by the employment of a
    personalized system which is dissimilar to other in-
    stitutions within the participating team network.

4. The inability of personalized systems to compare
    favorably with Library of Congress cards in terms of
    dependability, accuracy, and comprehensiveness in the
    majority of cases.

The obvious fact remains that, despite the existence of the
above disadvantages, any library which is willing to commit

itself to a cataloging scheme of its own devising may well
come up with an alternative which qualifies as vastly superior
to the systems which are presently in widespread use. Errors
can be minimized by care in planning and checking up on cleri-
cal work. Consistency can be built into a system through the
judicious application of trial testing periods which could aid
in the identification of any flaws in the original plan. Close
interaction between libraries in the planning stage of any
cooperative endeavor concerning itself with the cataloging,
acquisition, and lending functions should enable them to mini-
mize the problem of standardization.

CATALOGING MODELS

Examples of both unit entries and the main-entry system, estab-
lished through recourse to the *Anglo-American Cataloging Rules,*
are provided below:

Unit Entries

      Popular music "A Salty Dog." Pref. by
        Procol Harum. A&M 4179.
        12" LPS
        Contents: "A Salty Dog" "The Milk of
        Human Kindness" "Too Much Between Us"
        "The Devil Came from Kansas" "Boredom"
        "Juicy John Pink" "Wreck of the Hesperus"
        "All This and More" "Crucifiction Lane"
        "Pilgrims Progress."
        1. Procol Harum, rock group. 2. Rock groups.*

      Piano Concerto in A Minor, Op. 16, by Edvard
      Grieg. Perf. by Dinu Lipatti, piano; Alceo

    *This heading represents a makeshift creation in that it
    is not a part of the Library of Congress or Sears scheme
    of subject headings.

Galliera cond. Philharmonia Orchestra.
Odyssey 32 16 0141.
Side 1, 12" LPM
With Piano Concerto in A Minor, Op. 54, by
Robert Schumann.

1. Grieg, Edvard, 1844-1907. 2. Lipatti,
Dinu, piano. 3. Galliera, Alceo cond.
Philharmonia Orchestra. 4. Philharmonia
Orchestra cond. by Alceo Galliera.

Brief-Form of the Unit Entry

Procol Harum: "A Salty Dog." A&M SP 4179.

Main-Entry System (as outlined in the Anglo-American Cataloging Rules and employed by the Library of Congress):

A Salty Dog. (Phonodisc)
A&M SP 4179 (1969).
2s. 12 in. 33 1/3 rpm imcrogroove. Stereophonic.
Popular songs: Procol Harum (rock group) with
orchestral arrangements.
1. Music, Popular (Songs, etc.) Great Britain.
I. Procol Harum, rock group.

Grieg, Edvard, 1844-1907.
(Concerto, Piano, Op. 16, A Minor) Phonodisc.
Piano Concerto in A Minor, Op. 16.
Odyssey 32 16 0141. (1967)
1s. 12 in. 33 1/3 rpm microgroove (legendary performances)
Dinu Lipatti, piano; Philharmonia Orchestra; Alceo
Galliera, conductor.
Program notes in slipcase.
With: Schumann, Robert. Piano Concerto in A Minor, OP. 54.
1. Concerti. I. Lipatti, Dinu. II. Philharmonia
Orchestra. London. III. Galliera, Alceo.
IV. Title.

An example of the added entry (in this case as part of the main
entry system) is outlined below:

Music, Popular (Songs, Etc.) Great Britain

A Salty Dog. (Phonodisc)
A&M SP 4179 (1969).
2s. 12 in. 33 1/3 rpm microgroove. Stereophonic.
Popular songs: Procol Harum (rock group)
with orchestral arrangements.

NOTES

Osburn, Andrew D., "The crisis in cataloging," *Reader in Classification and Descriptive Cataloging* (Ann F. Painter, ed.), NCR Microcard Editions, Washington, D.C., 1972, p. 195.

Jay E. Daily, *Cataloging Phonorecordings: Problems and Possibilities,* Marcel Dekker, New York, 1975.

3. *Ibid.,* pp. 13-34.

    Ibid., pp. 33-34.

5. *Ibid.,* p. 140.

Chapter 7

A BASIC RECORDED SOUND COLLECTION

INTRODUCTION

This collection is meant to serve merely as a foundation; each
type of library ideally ought to carry a greater amount of
records and tapes than is recommended here. Libraries should
be encouraged to develop in various areas with a greater degree
of depth depending upon their respective needs, inclinations,
and capabilities. All of the entries listed here are recommended for both large public libraries and university libraries.
One star (*) will indicate recordings that should be included
in medium-sized public libraries and college libraries, as well
as in the collections of the larger institutions. Two stars
(**) will signify that the recording is also recommended for
(a) small public libraries, (b) school libraries and media
centers, and (c) institutional collections. The numerical to-
tals for these recommended holdings are as follows:

    Small public libraries, school libraries, etc.   313
    Medium-sized public libraries, college libraries   625
    Large public libraries, university libraries   1250

Double albums, boxed sets, etc., have all been included here
as one unit. Many of these titles are available in one or more
of the tape formats; libraries should select the particular
format(s) best suited to their respective purposes. The cost
to be incurred (taking into account the typical discounts given
off of retail prices) will be approximately $1600, $3200, and
$6400, respectively. Careful shopping habits (e.g., the exploi-
tation of alternative buying sources) could result in cutting
these costs by more than 50 percent.

The Schwann catalogs can not only be utilized as a means
of determining the formats in which a given release is available, but also as aids in determining which recordings are still
available. It is presumed on the part of the author that some
of the channels for the acquisition of out-of-print discs and
tapes, such as flea markets and specialty retail outlets, will
be utilized by librarians frequently.

The classical music entries included in this stock list
will provide less of a problem for the acquisition of in-print
recordings than will be the case with popular works. The
reason for this is that the classical music entries have been
entered by composition rather than by a specific recording, as
characterizes the popular music entries. In most cases, one
can select from more than one in-print recording of a classical
work at any given time.

No 45-rpm discs were included for the following reasons:

1. The rapidity with which these recordings tend to go
    out-of-print.

2. The availability of many of these selections in the
    long-playing album format.

3. The vast complexity of this sector. An incredible
    number of these discs have been released; many under
    obscure circumstances with a lack of appreciation for
    their true aesthetic worth. In short, to collect
    45-rpm discs requires a far deeper knowledge of the

popular music area (few 45's contain classical works, drama, etc.) than would be necessary merely to select a representative list of albums or tapes.

The criteria employed by the author in the compilation of this listing are those outlined in Chapter 2.

RECOMMENDED HOLDINGS

BLUES, RHYTHM AND BLUES

BLAND, Bobby. *Introspective Early Years.* 2-Duke.

HOOKER, John Lee. *Best.* 2-GNP.

HOWLIN' WOLF. *AKA Cnester Burnett.* 2-Chess.

JOHNSON, Blind Willie. *Blind Willie Johnson, 1927-1930.* Folkways.

JOHNSON, Robert. *King of the Delta Blues Singers, Volume II.* Columbia.*

KING, B.B. *Live at Cook County Jail.* ABC.**

LEADBELLY (aka Huddie Ledbetter). *Take This Hammer.* Folkways.

MCGHEE, Brownie. *Brownie McGhee/Sonny Terry: Preachin' the Blues.* Folkways.

MAGIC SAM BLUES BAND. *West Side Soul.* Delmark.

SLEEPY JOHN ESTES. *Sleepy John Estes, 1929-1940.* Folkways.

VARIOUS ARTISTS. *History of British Blues, Volume 1.* 2-Sire.*

WATERS, Muddy (aka McKinley Morganfield). *Fathers and Sons.* 2-Chess.*

WILLIAMSON, Sonny Boy. *My Story.* Chess.

CLASSICAL MUSIC: CHAMBER WORKS

BARTOK, Bela.
Quartet No. 2 in A Minor, Op. 17.

BEETHOVEN, Ludwig Van.
*Archduke Trio, Op. 97.** Grosse Fuge, Op. 133.* Quartet in A Minor, Op. 132.** Quartet in B Flat Major, Op. 130.* Quartet in C Sharp Minor, Op. 131.* Quartet in F Major, Op. 135.* String Quartet, Op. 18 (6). String Quartets, Op. 59 (3).*

BLOCH, Ernest.
Quartet in B Minor.

BORODIN, Alexander.
Quartet No. 2 in D Major.

BRAHMS, Johannes.
Quintet for Clarinet and Strings in B Minor, Op. 115.*
Quintet for Strings in F Major, Op. 88. Quintet for
Strings in G Major, Op. 111. Trio for Clarinet, Cello,
and Piano, Op. 114.*

COPLAND, Aaron.
Sonata for Violin and Piano.

DVORAK, Antonin.
Quartet No. 6 in F Major ("American"), Op. 96.* Quintet
for Piano and Strings in A Major, Op. 81. Trio for Piano
and Strings in F Minor, Op. 65.

FAURE, Gabriel.
Quartet, Op. 121.

HANDEL, George Frideric.
Trio Sonata in G Minor, Op. 5, No. 5.

HAYDN, Franz Joseph.
String Quartets, Op. 20. String Quartets, Op. 55. String
Quartet, Op. 75, No. 2.** String Quartets, Op. 76.**
String Quartet, Op. 77, No. 2.*

HINDEMITH, Paul.
Kleine Kammermusik, Op. 24, No. 2.

MOZART, Wolfgang Amadeus.
Divertimento in B Flat Major, K. 287. Divertimento in
D Major, K. 334. Divertimento in E Flat Major, K. 563.**
Duet in B Flat Major for Violin and Viola, K. 424.
Quartet in F Major (Oboe and Strings), K. 370. Quartet
in C Major, K. 465.* Quintet in C Major for Strings,
K. 515. Quintet in A Major for Clarinet and Strings,
K. 581. Serenade in B Flat Major for 13 Woodwinds, K. 361.

PISTEN, Walter.
Divertimento for 9 Instruments.

POULENC, Francis.
Sextet for Piano and Woodwind Quintet.

PURCELL, Henry.
Sonata in A Minor (Set 11, No. 3).

RAVEL, Maurice.
Introduction and Allegro for Harp, Flute, Clarinet and
String Quartet.

ROUSSEL, Albert.
Serenade for Flute, Violin, Viola, Cello and Harp.

SCHUBERT, Franz.
Octet in F Major. Quartet No. 14 in D Minor ("Death and the Maiden").** Quartet No. 15 in G Major. Quintet in A Major ("Trout").** Trio for Piano and Strings in B Flat Major, Op. 99.*

SCHUMANN, Robert.
Quartet for Piano and Strings in E Flat Major, Op. 47.

SHOSTAKOVICH, Dmitri.
Quintet for Piano and Strings, Op. 57.

STRAVINSKY, Igor.
L'Histoire du Soldat, Septet.** Octet for Wind Instruments.* Ragtime for 11 Instruments.

TCHAIKOVSKY, Peter.
Quartet in D Major, Op. 11.

VARESE, Edgard.
Ionisation, for Percussion Ensemble.

VILLA-LOBOS, Heitor.
Bachionas No. 6, Flute and Bassoon.

CLASSICAL MUSIC: KEYBOARD WORKS

BACH, Johann Christian.
Concerti (37) for Clavier.

BACH, Johann Sebastian.
Chorale Preludes for Organ: "Das Orgelbuchlein," S. 599-644.* Concerti (8) for Harpsichord, S. 1052/9. French Suites (6) for Harpsichord, S. 812/7.* Goldberg Variations for Harpsichord, S. 988.** Partitas (6) for Harpsichord, S. 825/30. Passacaglia and Fugue in C Minor for Organ, S. 582. Pastorale in F Major for Organ, S. 590. Preludes and Fugues for Organ, S. 531/52. Toccata and Fugue in D Minor for Organ, S. 565.** Toccata and Fugue in D Minor for Organ, S. 538 ("Dorian").* Well-Tempered Clavier, S. 846/93.**

BEETHOVEN, Ludwig Van.
Bagatelles, Op. 33; 119; 126. Concerti (5) for Piano and Orchestra.** Sonatas (32) for Piano.**

BRAHMS, Johannes.
Ballades (4), Op. 10. Concerto No. 2 in B Flat for Piano and Orchestra, Op. 83.* Intermezzi, Op. 76; 116; 117; 118; 119. Rhapsodies, Op. 79. Scherzo in E Flat Minor, Op. 4.

BUXTEHUDE, Dietrich.
Suites (19) for Klavier.

BYRD, William.
  Keyboard Musick.

CHOPIN, Frederic.
  Ballades, Op. 23; 38; 47; 52.**   Concerto No. 1 in E Minor,
  Op. 11. Concerto No. 2 in F minor, Op. 21. Etudes,
  Op. 10; 25.**   Impromptus (4).*   Mazurkas (51).**
  Nocturnes (21).**   Polonaises (8).**   Preludes (24),
  Op. 28.**   Scherzi, Op. 20; 31; 39; 54.**   Sonata No. 2
  in B Flat, Op. 35.*   Waltzes.

DEBUSSY, Claude.
  Arabesques (2).**   Preludes for Piano, Books 1 and 2.

FRANCK, Cesar.
  Chorales (3) for Organ.**   Partorale for Organ.   Prelude,
  Chorale et Fugue for Piano.   Symphonic Variations for
  Piano and Orchestra.**

GERSHWIN, George.
  Concerto in F Major for Piano.*   Rhapsody in Blue.**

GRIEG, Edvard.
  Concerto in A Minor for Piano and Orchestra.**   Lyric
  Pieces (10 sets), Op. 12; 38; 43; 47; 54; 57; 62; 65; 68;
  71.*

HANDEL, George Frideric.
  Concerti (16) for Organ.   Suites for Harpsichord.

HAYDN, Franz Joseph.
  Andante Con Variazioni in F Minor.   Concerti (3) in
  C Major for Organ.   Sonatas for Piano.

LISZT, Franz.
  Concerto No. 2 in A Major for Piano and Orchestra.**
  Hungarian Rhapsodies (19) for Piano.*   Liebestraum No. 2
  in A Flat Major.   Transcendental Etudes (12).

MENDELSSOHN, Felix.
  Concerto No. 1 in G Minor for Piano, Op. 25.   Songs
  Without Words (Op. 19b; 30; 38; 53; 62; 67; 85; 102).

MOZART, Wolfgang Amadeus.
  Concerti (25) for Piano and Orchestra.**   Sonatas (17)
  for Organ and Orchestra.   Sonatas (17) for Piano.**

PADEREWSKI, Ignace.
  Concerto in A Minor for Piano and Orchestra.

PROKOFIEV, Serge.
  Concerto No. 2 for Piano, Op. 16.*   Concerto No. 3 for
  Piano, Op. 26.   Concerto No. 5 for Piano, Op. 55.   Sonatas
  for Piano.

PURCELL, Henry.
   Suites for Harpsichord.

RACHMANINOFF, Sergei.
   *Concerto No. 2 in C Major for Piano, Op. 18.** Concerto
   No. 3 in D Minor for Piano, Op. 30.* Etudes-Tableaux,
   Op. 33, 39. Preludes for Piano, Op. 23, 32.*

RAVEL, Maurice.
   Concerto in D Major for the Left Hand. Concerto in
   G Major for Piano and Orchestra. Gaspard de lanuit.
   Pavane pour une infante defunte.*

SATIE, Erik.
   Gnossiennes (6).

SCHUBERT, Franz.
   Impromptus, Op. 90; 142. Marches Militaires (3), Op. 51.

SCHUMANN, Robert.
   Arabeske for Piano, Op. 18. Carnaval, Op. 9.**
   Concerto in A Major for Piano and Orchestra, Op. 54.**
   Fantasiestucke, Op. 12. Kreisleriana, Op. 16.*

ACRIABIN, Alexander.
   Etudes (12), Op. 8.* Sonatas (10) for Piano.

TCHAIKOVSKY, Peter.
   *Concerto No. 1 for Piano and Orchestra, Op. 23.**
   Concerto No. 3 for Piano and Orchestra, Op. 75.*

TELEMANN, Georg Philipp.
   Fantasias (36) for Clavier.*

WEBER, Carl Maria Von.
   Rondo Brilliante (Invitation to the Dance), Op. 65.

CLASSICAL MUSIC: STRING AND WOODWIND WORKS

BACH, Johann Sebastian.
   *Brandenburg Concerti (6), S. 1046/51.** Concerti (2) for
   Violin, S. 1041/2.* Concerto in D Minor for 2 Violins,
   S. 1043.** Concerto in A Minor for Flute, Violin and
   Harpsichord, S. 1044. Sonatas (3) and Partitas (3) for
   Violin Unaccompanied, S. 1001/6. Sonatas (6) for Violin
   and Harpsichord, S. 1014/19. Suites for Cello Unaccom-
   panied, S. 1007/12.*

BEETHOVEN, Ludwig Van.
   Concerto in D Major for Violin, Op. 61. Sonatas (10)
   for Violin and Piano.**

BERLIOZ, Hector.
   Harold in Italy.**

BLOCH, Ernest.
Schelomo--Hebrew Rhapsody for Cello and Orchestra.

BRAHMS, Johannes.
Concerto in D Major for Violin, Op. 77.** *Concerto in A Minor for Violin and Cello, Op. 102.* Sonatas in E Minor and F Major for Cello and Piano, Op. 38; 99. Sonatas (3) for Violin and Piano, Op. 78; 100; 108.*

BRUCH, Max.
Concerto No. 1 in G Minor for Violin, Op. 26.* Scottish Fantasy for Violin and Orchestra, Op. 46.**

CHAUSSON, Ernest.
Poeme for Violin and Orchestra, Op. 25.

CORELLI, Arcangelo.
Concerto Grosso in G Minor ("Christmas Concerto").

DVORAK, Antonin.
Concerto in B Minor for Cello, Op. 104.

FRANCK, Cesar.
Sonata in A Major for Violin and Piano.

GEMINIANI, Francesco.
Concerti Grossi (6), Op. 3.

HANDEL, George Frideric.
Concerti (3) for Oboe. Concerti Grossi (12), Op.6. Concerto in B Flat for Harp and Orchestra, Op. 4, No. 6.* Sonatas, Op. 1 for Flute (7). Sonatas, Op. 1 for Violin (6).

HAYDN, Franz Joseph.
Concerto in E Flat for Trumpet and Orchestra.

HINDEMITH, Paul.
Sonata for Viola (Unaccompanied), Op. 25, No. 1. Sonata for Unaccompanied Cello, Op. 25, No. 3.

LALO, Edouard.
Symphonie Espagnole for Violin and Orchestra, Op. 21.**

LOCATELLI, Pietro.
Concerti Grossi (12), Op. 1.

MENDELSSOHN, Felix.
Concerto in E Minor for Violin and Orchestra, Op. 64.*

MOZART, Wolfgang Amadeus.
Concerti (4) for Horn, K. 412, 417, 447, 495.** *Concerto in A Major for Clarinet, K. 622.* Concerto No. 1 in G Major for Flute, K. 313. Sinfonia Concertante in E Flat for Oboe, Clarinet, Bassoon, Horn and Strings,*

K. Anh. 9 (297b).** Sinfonia Concertante in E Flat for Violin and Viola, K. 364.* Sonatas (42) for Violin and Piano.

PAGANINI, Niccolo.
Caprices (24) for Unaccompanied Violin, Op. 1.** Concerto No. 1 in D Major for Violin, Op. 6. Moto Perpetuo, Op. 11.

PERGOLESI, Giovanni Battista.
Sonata for Violin and Strings.

PROKOFIEV, Serge.
Concerto in D Major for Violin and Orchestra, Op. 19.
Concerto in G Minor for Violin and Orchestra, Op. 63.

PURCELL, Henry.
Sonata in D Major for Trumpet and Strings.*

RAVEL, Maurice.
Tzigane, Rhapsodie de Concert for Violin and Piano.

SAINT-SAENS, Camille.
Introduction and Rhondo Capriccio for Violin and Orchestra, Op. 28.

SCARLATTI, Alessandro.
Sinfonia No. 2 in D Major for Flute, Trumpet and Strings.

SCHUBERT, Franz.
Sonata in A Major for Violin and Piano, Op. 162, D. 574.*

SCHUMANN, Robert.
Concerto in A Minor for Cello and Orchestra, Op. 129.*
Romances (3) for Oboe, Op. 94.

SIBELIUS, Jean.
Concerto in D Minor for Violin and Orchestra, Op. 47.

TCHAIKOVSKY, Peter.
Concerto in D Major for Violin and Orchestra, Op. 35.**

VIVALDI, Antonio.
Concerti for Flute and Orchestra. Concerti for Piccolo.
Concerti for 2 Violins and Orchestra.* Concerto for 2 Trumpets, P. 75.*

CLASSICAL MUSIC: SYMPHONIC WORKS

BACH, Johann Sebastian.
Brandenburg Concerti (6).** Concerto in D Minor for 2 Violins, S. 1043.**

BALAKIREV, Mily.
Islamey (Oriental Fantasy).

BEETHOVEN, Ludwig Van.
   Coriolanus Overture. Egmont Overture. Fidelio Overture;
   Leonore Overtures (3). Prometheus Overture. Symphonies.**

BERLIOZ, Hector.
   "Le Carnaval Romain" Overture.* *Romeo and Juliet (Dramatic*
   Symphony).* *Symphonie Fantastique.***

BIŽET, Georges.
   L'Arlesienne: Suites 1 and 2.

BORODIN, Alexander.
   Symphony No. 2 in B Minor.**

BRAHMS, Johannes.
   Symphonies No. 1-4.** *Tragic Overture.** *Variations on a*
   Theme by Haydn, Op. 56a.**

BRUCKNER, Anton.
   Symphony No. 3.** *Symphony No. 4.** *Symphony No. 5.***
   Symphony No. 6.** *Symphony No. 7.*

CHABRIER, Emmanuel.
   Espana.

COPLAND, Aaron.
   Appalachian Spring: Suite. Billy the Kid: Suite. Fanfare
   for the Common Man. Rodeo: Ballet Suite.

DEBUSSY, Claude.
   Images pour Orchestre (3). La Mer.* *Nocturnes (Nuages,*
   Fetes, Sirenes).* *Prelude a l'apres-midi d'un faune.***

DELIUS, Frederick.
   In a Summer Garden; On Hearing the First Cuckoo in Spring.

DUKAS, Paul.
   The Sorcerer's Apprentice.**

DVORAK, Antonin.
   Slavonic Dances, Op. 46; 72. Symphony No. 7.* *Symphony*
   No. 8.* *Symphony No. 9.**

ELGAR, Edward.
   Variations on an Original Theme ("Enigma"), Op. 36.*

FRANCK, Cesar.
   Les Eolides. Psyche.** *Symphonic Variations for Piano*
   and Orchestra. Symphony in D Minor.**

GEMINIANI, Francesco.
   The Enchanted Forest.

GRIEG, Edvard.
   Norwegian Dances, Op. 35 (4). Peer Gynt Suites, 1 and 2.**

HANDEL, George Frideric.
Royal Fireworks Music.* Water Music.**

HARRIS, Roy.
Symphony No. 3. When Johnny Comes Marching Home (An American Overture).

HAYDN, Franz Joseph.
Symphony No. 45 ("Farewell"). Symphonies No. 92-104.**

HOLST, Gustav.
The Planets.**

HONEGGER, Arthur.
Pacific 231.

IPPOLITOV-IVANOV, Mikhail.
Caucasian Sketches.

IVES, Charles.
Symphonies No. 1-4.* Three Places in New England.

LIADOV, Anatol.
Baba Yaga, Op. 56; Enchanted Lake; 8 Russian Folksongs, Op. 58.

LISZT, Franz.
A Faust Symphony.**

MACDOWELL, Edward.
Suite No. 2 ("Indian").

MAHLER, Gustav.
Symphony No. 2.** Symphony No. 4.** Symphony No. 8.* Symphony No. 9.*

MENDELSSOHN, Felix.
The Hebrides Overture ("Fingel's Cave").** Incidental Music to "A Midsummer Night's Dream."** Symphony No. 3.** Symphony No. 4.**

MOZART, Wolfgang Amadeus.
Eine Kleine Nachtmusik.** Symphony No. 34. Symphony No. 35. Symphony No. 36. Symphony No. 38.** Symphony No. 39.** Symphony No. 40.** Symphony No. 41.**

MUSSORGSKY, Modest.
Night on Bare Mountain.** Pictures at an Exhibition.**

PROKOFIEV, Serge.
Alexander Nevsky, Op. 78.** Classical Symphony, Op. 25.* Lieutenant Kije, Op. 60.** Symphony No. 5, Op. 100.**

PURCELL, Henry.
Sonata in D for Trumpet and Strings.

RACHMANINOFF, Serge.
  Isle of the Dead, Op. 29. Symphony No. 2, Op. 27.*

RAVEL, Maurice.
  *Bolero.** Mother Goose Suite. Rhapsodie Espagnole.
  Le Tombeau de Couperin. Le Valse.**

RESPIGHI, Ottorino.
  *Festivals of Rome.** Fountains of Rome.** Pines of
  Rome.***

RIMSKY-KORSAKOV, Nikolai.
  Capriccio Espagnole, Op. 34. "Russian Easter" Overture,
  Op. 36. Scheherazade, Symphonic Suite, Op. 35.**
  Symphony No. 2, "Antar," Op. 9.***

ROSSINI, Gioacchino.
  Overtures.

ROUSSEL, Albert.
  Bacchus et Ariane, Op. 43.

RUBENSTEIN, Anton.
  Symphony No. 2 ("Ocean").*

SAINT-SAENS, Camille.
  Carnival of Animals.* Symphony No. 3 ("Organ").

SATIE, Erik.
  Trois Gymnopedies.

SCHOENBERG, Arnold.
  Five Pieces for Orchestra.* Verklarte Nacht, Op. 4.*

SCHUBERT, Franz.
  *Symphony No. 4. Symphony No. 5. Symphony No. 8.**
  Symphony No. 9.**

SCHUMANN, Robert.
  Symphony No. 3.* Symphony No. 4.*

SCRIABIN, Alexander.
  Symphony No. 3.* Symphony No. 4.* Symphony No. 5.*

SHOSTAKOVICH, Dmitri.
  *Symphony No. 1. Symphony No. 2. Symphony No. 5.**
  Symphony No. 6. Symphony No. 7. Symphony No. 10.*
  Symphony No. 15.*

SIBELIUS, Jean.
  *Finlandia, Op. 26.** Four Legends from the Kalevala,
  Op. 22. Karelia Suite, Op. 11. Symphony No. 2.
  Symphony No. 5.* Symphony No. 7.*

SMETANA, Bedrich.
  The Moldau.** My Fatherland.*

STRAUSS, Johann.
> *Waltzes,* particularly: *Blue Danube; Emperor Waltz; Voices of Spring; Wiener Blut; Wine, Women and Song; Tales from Vienna Woods.*

STRAUSS, Richard.
> *Death and Transfiguration.* Don Juan.* Don Quixote.* Ein Heldenleben. Thus Spake Zarathustra.** Till Eulunspiegel's Merry Pranks.***

STRAVINSKY, Igor.
> *Symphony of Psalms.*

TCHAIKOVSKY, Peter.
> *Capriccio Italien, Op. 45.** "1812" Overture.** Francesca Da Rimini (Symphonic Fantasy), Op. 32.** Marche Slav, Op. 31.** Symphony No. 1. Symphony No. 2. Symphony No. 4.** Symphony No. 5.** Symphony No. 6.** Symphony, "Manfred."**

TELEMANN, Georg Philipp.
> *Concerto in D Major for 3 Trumpets, 2 Oboes and Orchestra.* Suite in F for 4 Hornsm 2 Oboes and String Orchestra.***

TORELLI, Giuseppe.
> *Concerto in D Major for Trumpet and Orchestra.*

VAUGHN WILLIAMS, Ralph.
> *Fantasia on a Theme by Tallis. Fantasia on "Greensleeves." Symphony No. 1 ("Sea").* Symphony No. 2 ("London").* Symphony No. 4.* Symphony No. 7 ("Antarctica").* Symphony No. 9.* The Wasps, Overture.*

VIVALDI, Antonio.
> *Four Seasons, Op. 8.***

WAGNER, Richard.
> *Siegfried Idyll.***

WALTON, William.
> *Facade.*

CLASSICAL MUSIC: VOCAL WORKS

BACH, Carl Philipp Emanuel.
> *Magnificat.*

BACH, Johann Sebastian.
> *Cantata No. 4, Christ lag in Todesbanden. Cantata No. 202, Welchet nur ("Wedding Cantata").* Cantata No. 212, "Peasant Cantata."* Christmas Oratorio, S. 248. Magnificat in D Major, D. 243.* Mass in B Minor, S. 232.** St. John Passion. St. Matthew Passion.***

BEETHOVEN, Ludwig Van.
*Missa Solemnis in D Major, Op. 123.***

BERLIOZ, Hector.
*Te Deum, Op. 22.**

BRAHMS, Johannes.
*Alto Rhapsody, Op. 53.*** *Ernste Gesange. A German Requiem, Op. 45.***

BRITTEN, Benjamin.
*Ceremony of Carols, Op. 28.** *War Requiem, Op. 66.***

BRUCKNER, Anton.
Mass No. 2 in E Minor. Mass No. 3 in F Minor, the "Great." Te Deum.

BUXTEHUDE, Dietrich.
*Cantatas.***

BYRD, William.
*Madrigals, Motets, Anthems.**

DEBUSSY, Claude.
*Fetes Galantes, Nos. 1 and 2 (Song Cycles).** *Songs.**

DES PRES, Josquin.
Motets.

DOWLAND, John.
Ayres (3 Books).

FAURE, Gabriel.
*Requiem, Op. 48.**

GRETRY, Andre.
Arias.

HANDEL, George Frideric.
Cantatas.

HAYDN, Franz Joseph.
Mass No. 9 in D Minor, Missa Solemnis ("Nelson Mass").

LASSUS, Orlandus (Roland de).
*Madrigals.*** *Motets.**

MAHLER, Gustav.
*Das Lied von der Erde.** *Songs of a Wayfarer.*

MONTEVERDI, Claudio.
*Madrigals.*** *Vespro della Beata Vergine.*

MORLEY, Thomas.
Madrigals.

MOZART, Wolfgang Amadeus.
Mass in C Major, K. 317 ("Coronation").* Mass in C Minor, K. 427 ("the Great").* Requiem, K. 626.**

MUSSORGSKY, Modest.
Songs and Dances of Death (Song Cycle).

PALESTRINA, Giovanni.
Missa Assumpta Est Maria. Motets.**

PERGOLESI, Giovanni Battista.
Stabat Mater.

POULENC, Francis.
Songs.

PROKOFIEV, Serge.
Peter and the Wolf, Op. 67.**

SCHOENBERG, Arnold.
Gurre-Lieder. Pierrot Lunaire, Op. 21.

SCHUBERT, Franz.
Der Erlkonig, Op. 1.** Die Schone Mullerin, Op. 25 (Song Cycle). Der Doppelganger (Schwanengesang No. 13).

SCHUMANN, Robert.
Dichterliebe, Op. 48 (Song Cycle). Liederkreis, Op. 39 (Song Cycle).

SCHUTZ, Heinrich.
Psalms.

TCHAIKOVSKY, Peter.
Songs.

TELEMANN, Georg Philipp.
Cantatas.

VERDI, Giuseppe.
Requiem Mass.**

VICTORIA, Tomas Luis de.
Motets and Choral Works.

WOLF, Hugo.
Songs.*

COUNTRY AND WESTERN

ANDERSON, Bill. *Scorpio.* MCA.

ANDERSON, Lynn. *Hits, Volume 2.* Columbia.

ATKINS, Chet and Merle Travis. *Traveling Show.* RCA.

BLUE RIDGE RANGERS. *Blue Ridge Rangers.* Fantasy.

CASH, Johnny. *Folsom and San Quentin.* 2-Columbia.

FENDER, Freddy. *Best of Freddy Fender.* Dot.

FLATT AND SCRUGGS. *World.* Columbia.

HAGGARD, Merle. *Best of the Best.* Capitol.**

HALL, Tom T. *Hits, Volume 2.* Mercury.

JENNINGS, Waylon. *This Time.* RCA.**

JONES, George. *The Race Is On.* Camden.

LYNN, Loretta. *Greatest Hits, Volume 2.* MCA.

MANDRELL, Barbara. *Best of Barbara Mandrell.* Columbia.

MONROE, Bill. *Best of Bill Monroe.* 2-MCA.*

NELSON, Willie. *Best of Willie Nelson.* United Artists.

OWENS, Buck. *Best of Buck Owens, Volume 6.* Capitol.

PARTON, Dolly. *Best of Dolly Parton.* RCA.*

PRIDE, Charley. *Best of Charley Pride, Volume 3.* RCA.*

REEVES, Jim. *Distant Drums.* RCA.*

RICH, Charlie. *Behind Closed Doors.* Epic.**

ROBBINS, Marty. *All-Time Greatest Hits.* 2-Columbia.

RODGERS, Jimmie. *My Rough and Rowdy Ways.* RCA.*

SNOW, Hank. *No. 104: Still Movin' On.* RCA.

TUBB, Ernest. *Ernest Tubb.* MCA.

TUCKER, Tanya. *Lovin' and Learnin'.* MCA.

TWITTY, Conway. *Greatest Hits, Volume II.* MCA.

VARIOUS ARTISTS. *Country Hits of the '60's.* Capitol.*

VARIOUS ARTISTS. *Country Love, Volume 2.* 2-Columbia.

WILLIAMS, Hank. *24 Greatest Hits.* 2-MGM.*

WILLS, Bob. *Anthology.* Columbia.

WYNETTE, Tammy. *I Still Believe in Fairy Tales.* Epic.

DRAMA

AESCHYLUS.
   Agamemnon. Prometheus Bound.
CHEKHOV, Anton.
   *Cherry Orchard. Three Sisters.**
EURIPIDES.
   Electra. The Medea.

IBSEN, Henrik.
    *A Doll's House.**

MOLIERE.
    *Misanthrope.**   *Tartuffe.*

O'NEILL, Eugene.
    *Emperor Jones.**

ROSTAND, Edmond.
    Cyrano de Bergerac.

SARTRE, Jean Paul.
    No Exit.

SHAKESPEARE, William.
    *Hamlet.**   *Henry VIII.   Julius Caesar.   King Lear.**
    *Macbeth.**   *Merchant of Venice.   Merry Wives of Windsor.*
    *A Midsummer Night's Dream.**   *Much Ado About Nothing.*
    *Othello.   Pericles.   Richard III.   Romeo and Juliet.**
    Taming of the Shrew.   Twelfth Night.   Winter's Tale.

SHAW, George Bernard.
    *Major Barbara.   Pygmalion.**

SOPHOCLES.
    *Antigone.   Oedipus Rex.**

WILLIAMS, Tennessee.
    *Glass Menagerie.   Streetcar Named Desire.**

FOLK

BAEZ, Joan. *Any Day Now.* Vanguard.**

CARTER FAMILY. *Green Fields of Virginia.* RCA.*

DYER-BENNETT, Richard. *Essential.* 2-Vanguard.

ELLIOT, Ramblin' Jack. *Essential.* 2-Vanguard.

GUTHRIE, Woody. *This Land Is Your Land.* Folkways.**

HOUSTON, Cisco. *Cisco Houston Sings American Folk Songs.*
    Folkways.

KINCAID, Bradley. *Mountain Ballads and Old Time Songs; Album
    No. 3.* Bluebonnet.

NEW LOST CITY RAMBLERS. *Modern Times.* Folkways.

OCHS, Phil. *Chords of Fame.* 2-A&M.

PETER, PAUL AND MARY. *In the Wind.* Warner Brothers.*

RITCHIE, Jean. *None But One.* Sire.

RONK, Dave Van. *Black Mountain Blues.* Folkways.

SAINTE-MARIE, Buffy. *Sweet America.* ABC.

SEEGER, Mike. *Music From the True Vine.* Mercury.

SEEGER, Pete. *Pete Seeger At the Village Gate.* Folkways.*

WATSON, Doc. *Elementary Doctor Watson.* Poppy.*

WEAVERS. *Greatest Hits.* Decca.*

WEST, Harry and Jeannie. *Songs of the Southland.* Folkways.

JAZZ

ADDERLEY, Julian "Cannonball." *Best.* Capitol.*

AMMONS, Gene. *Greatest Hits.* Prestige.

ARMSTRONG, Louis. *Best.* Audio Fidelity.** *Louis "Satchmo" Armstrong.* Archive of Folk Music.*

BARBIERI, Gato. *Chapter I--Latin America.* Impulse.

BASIE, Count. *Echoes of an Era.* 2-Roulette.** *Echoes of an Era (Vocal Years).* 2-Roulette.**

BENSON, George. *Bad Benson.* CTI. *Breezin'.* Warner Brothers.*

BLACKBYRDS. *Flying Start.* Fantasy.

BLAKE, Eubie. *86 Years of Eubie Blake.* 2-Columbia.

BRAXTON, Anthony. *3 Compositions.* Delmark.

BRUBECK, Dave. *All-Time Greatest Hits.* 2-Columbia.*

BURTON, Gary. *Alone At Last.* Atlantic.

BYRD, Charlie. *Brazilian Byrd.* Columbia.*

BYRD, Donald. *Street Lady.* Blue Note.**

CHARLES, Ray. *Best.* Atlantic.** *Genius After Hours.* Atlantic.

CLARKE, Stan. *Children of Forever.* Polydor.**

COBHAM, Billy. *Spectrum.* Atlantic.**

COLEMAN, Ornette. *Town Hall Concert.* ESP.

COLTRANE, John. *Best/Greatest Years.* Impulse.** *Blue Train.* Blue Note. *Giant Steps.* Atlantic.

CORYELL, Larry. *Introducing Eleventh House.* Vanguard.*

CRUSADERS. *Festival Album.* Pacific Jazz. *Southern Comfort.* 2-Blue Thumb.**

DAVIS, Miles. *Kind of Blue.* Columbia. *Sketches of Spain.* Columbia. *In A Silent Way.* Columbia.* *Bitches Brew.* 2-Columbia.**

DEODATO, Eumir. *Prelude.* CTI.**

DUKES OF DIXIELAND. *Best.* Audio Fidelity.

ELLINGTON, Duke. *Best.* Capitol.** *Echoes of an Era.*
  2-Roulette.* *Recollections of the Big Band Era.* Atlantic.

ELLIS, Don. *Electric Bath.* Columbia.

FITZGERALD, Ella. *History.* 2-Verve.**

GARNER, Errol. *Misty.* Mercury.

GETZ, Stan. *History.* 2-Verve.

GILLESPIE, Dizzy. *In the Beginning.* 2-Prestige.

GOODMAN, Benny. *All-Time Greatest Hits.* 2-Columbia.**

HANCOCK, Herbie. *Headhunters.* Columbia.**

HAWKINS, Coleman. *Reevaluations, Impulse Years.* 2-Impulse.

HERMAN, Woody. *Jazz Hoot.* Columbia.*

HINES, Earl. *At Home.* Delmark.

HODGES, Johnny. *Everybody Knows.* Impulse.

JARRETT, Keith. *Solo Concerts.* 3-ECM/Polydor.*

JONES, Elvin. *Impulse Years.* Impulse.

JONES, Quincy. *Body Heat.* A&M.*

JOPLIN, Scott. *Ragtime, Volume 3.* Biograph.*

KENTON, Stan. *Greatest Hits.* Capitol.*

LEWIS, Ramsey. *Best.* Cadet.* *Sun Goddess.* Columbia.**

MANGIONE, Chuck. *Land of Make Believe.* Mercury.*

MINGUS, Charlie. *Best.* Atlantic.

MODERN JAZZ QUARTET. *Blues on Bach.* Atlantic. *Best.*
  Atlantic.*

MONK, Thelonious. *Greatest Hits.* Columbia.*

MONTGOMERY, Wes. *A Day in the Life.* A&M.**

MULLIGAN, Gerry. *Paris Concert.* Pacific Jazz.*

NEW ORLEANS HERITAGE HALL JAZZ BAND. *New Orleans Heritage
  Hall Jazz Band.* DJ.

NEW ORLEANS RAGTIME ORCHESTRA. *New Orleans Ragtime Orchestra.*
  Arhoolie.

PARKER, Charlie. *Charlie Parker.* 2-Prestige.* *Echoes of an
  Era.* 2-Roulette.*

PONTY, Jean-Luc. *Electronic Connection.* Pacific Jazz.

RA, Sun. *Pathways to Unknown Worlds*. Impulse.

REINHARDT, Django. *Immortal*. Reprise.*

RUSHING, Jimmy. *Essential*. 2-Vanguard.

SCOTT-HERON, Gil. *First Minute of a New Day*. Arista.**

SHORTER, Wayne. *Super Nova*. Blue Note.**

SILVER, Horace. *Best*. Blue Note.

SMITH, Jimmy. *Got My Mojo Working*. Verve. *History*. 2-Verve.*

SMITH, Willie "the Lion." *Pork and Beans*. Black Lion.

SWINGLE SINGERS. *Bach's Hits*. Phillips.*

TURRENTINE, Stanley. *Pieces of Dreams*. Fantasy.**

TYNER, McCoy. *Reevaluation: Impulse Years*. 2-Impulse.

VAUGHN, Sarah. *Echoes of an Era*. 2-Roulette.**

WASHINGTON, Dinah. *Echoes of an Era*. 2-Roulette.*

WASHINGTON, Grover, Jr. *Inner City Blues*. Kudu.**

WEATHER REPORT. *Mysterious Traveler*. Columbia. *Sweetnighter*. Columbia.**

ZAWINUL, Joe. *Zawinul*. Atlantic.

Jazz Anthologies:

Big Bands: Brown, Gray, Ellington, Goodman, James, Herman. 6-Capitol.**

Decade of Jazz, Volume 1, 1939-49. 2-Blue Note.

Decade of Jazz, Volume 2, 1949-59. 2-Blue Note.

Decade of Jazz, Volume 3, 1959-69. 2-Blue Note.

Drums, The. 3-Impulse.*

Jazz Piano Anthology, A. 2-Columbia.

Piano Giants. 2-Prestige.**

Piano Roll Hall of Fame. Sounds.**

Ragtime Special. 2-Camden.*

MUSICALS, MOVIES, RADIO SHOWS

American Graffiti (Soundtrack). 2-MCA.**

Cabaret (Soundtrack). ABC.*

Camelot (Original Cast). Columbia.**

Captain Midnight (Radio). Mark 56.

Carousel (Soundtrack). Capitol.*

Clockwork Orange (Soundtrack). Warner Brothers.

Dr. Zhivago (Soundtrack). MGM.

Easy Rider (Soundtrack). MGM.

Fiddler on the Roof (Soundtrack). 2-United Artists.

Finian's Rainbow (Original Cast). RCA.

Gone With the Wind (Soundtrack). Warner Brothers.*

Great Gildersleeve/Our Miss Brooks (Radio). Radiola Company.

Hello Dolly (Original Cast). RCA.**

Jesus Christ Superstar (Original Cast). 2-MCA.**

King And I (Soundtrack). Capitol.

Lady Sings the Blues (Soundtrack). 2-Motown.*

Lenny (Original Cast). 2-Blue Thumb.

Little Orphan Annie (Radio). Mark 56.

Lone Ranger (Radio). Mark 56.*

Man of La Mancha (Original Cast). MCA.

Mary Poppins (Soundtrack). Buena Vista.*

Music Man (Soundtrack). Warner Brothers.**

My Fair Lady (Original Cast; first version). Columbia.*

Oklahoma (Soundtrack). Capitol.*

Pat Garrett and Billy the Kid (Soundtrack). Columbia.

1776 (Original Cast). Columbia.

Shadow (Radio). Mark 56.

Shaft (Soundtrack). Stax.**

Sound ofMusic (Soundtrack). RCA.**

South Pacific (Soundtrack). RCA.

Star Wars (Soundtrack). 2-20th Century Fox.**

Sting (Soundtrack). MCA.*

Superman (Radio). Mark 56.*

Tarzan (Radio). Mark 56.

2001: A Space Odyssey (Soundtrack). MGM.*

War of the Worlds (Radio). Radiola Company.*

West Side Story (Soundtrack). Columbia.*

Wizard of Oz (Soundtrack). MGM.

OPERA, OPERETTA, BALLET, ORATORIO

ADAM, Adolphe-Charles.
   Giselle (Ballet).**

BARTOK, Bela.
   Duke Bluebeard's Castle.

BEETHOVEN, Ludwig Van.
   *Fidelio.***

BELLINI, Vincenzo.
   *Norma.*** *Il Pirata. I Puritani de Scozia. La Sonnambula.**

BERG, Alban.
   *Wozzeck.***

BERLIOZ, Hector.
   Benvenuto Cellini. La Damnation de Faust (Dramatic
   Oratorio). *L'Enfance du Christ* (Oratorio).* *Les Troyen.***

BIZET, Georges.
   *Carmen.***

BLITZSTEIN, Marc.
   The Cradle Will Rock.

BLOW, John.
   Venus and Adonis.

BOITO, Arrigo.
   *Mefistofele.**

BORODIN, Alexander.
   *Prince Igor.***

BRITTEN, Benjamin.
   *Albert Herring.*** *Billy Budd. A Midsummer Night's Dream.***
   Owen Wingrave. *Parables: Burning Fiery Furnace; Curlew
   River; Prodigal Son. Peter Grimes.*** *Rape of Lucretia.*

CHARPENTIER, Gustave.
   Louise.

CHERUBINI, Luigi.
   Medee.

CILEA, Francesco.
   *Adriana Lecouvreur.**

CIMAROSA, Domenico.
   Matrimonio Segreto, Il.

DEBUSSY, Claude.
   Pelleas et Melisande.

DELIBES, Leo.
   Coppelia (Ballet).** *Sylvia* (Ballet).*

DELIUS, Frederick.
   A Village Romeo and Juliet.

DONIZETTI, Gaetano.
   Don Pasquale. L'Elisir d'amore. *La Favorite. La Fille
   du regiment.* *Lucia di Lammermoor.***

FLOTOW, Friedrich Von.
   Martha.

GERSHWIN, George.
   *Porgy and Bess.***

GILBERT AND SULLIVAN.
   *H.M.S. Pinafore.** *Mikado.** *Pirates of Penzance.***
   Sorceror.

GIORDANO, Umberto.
   Andrea Chenier.

GLUCK, Christoph Willibald Von.
   *Alceste. Orfeo ed Euridice.***

GOUNOD, Charles.
   *Faust.** *Romeo et Juliette.*

HANDEL, George Frideric.
   Acis and Galatea (Dramatic Masque). *Ariodante. Hercules.*
   Israel in Egypt (Oratorio).** *Judas Maccabaeus* (Oratorio).*
   Julius Caesar. Messiah (Oratorio).** *Samson* (Oratorio).
   Saul (Oratorio). *Solomon* (Oratorio). *Tamerlano.*

HAYDN, Franz Joseph.
   Creation (Oratorio).* *Seasons* (Oratorio). *Seven Last
   Words of Christ* (Oratorio).

HINDEMITH, Paul.
   Cardillac.

HONEGGER, Arthur.
   Le Roi David (Oratorio).

HUMPERDINCK, Engelbert.
   *Hansel und Gretel.***

JANACEK, Leos.
   Jenufa.

KODALY, Zoltan.
   Hary Janos.

LEONCAVALLO, Ruggero.
  *I Pagliacci.***

LORTZING, Gustav.
  Czar und Zimmerman.

MASCAGNI, Pietro.
  *Cavalleria Rusticana.***

MASSENET, Jules.
  Manon. *Werther.**

MENDELSSOHN, Felix.
  Elijah (Oratorio).

MENOTTI, Gian-Carlo.
  *Amahl and the Night Visitors.**

MEYERBEER, Giacomo.
  *Les Huguenots.**

MONTEVERDI, Claudio.
  *L'Incoronazione di Poppea. Orfeo.** Ritorno d'Ulisse.*

MOZART, Wolfgang Amadeus.
  *Cosi fan tutte.** Don Giovanni.** Die Entfuhrung aus dem
  Serail.* Idomeneo, Re di Creta. * Nozze di Figaro.** Die
  Zauberflote.***

MUSSORGSKY, Modest.
  *Boris Godunov.** Khovantchina.*

OFFENBACH, Jacques.
  *Contes d'Hoffmann.** Gaite Parisienne* (Ballet).*

ORFF, Carl.
  Antigone. Carmina Burana* (Dramatic Masque).** *Catulli
  Carmina* (Dramatic Masque). *Der Mond.*

PENDERECKI, Krzystof.
  Utrenja (Oratorio).*

PEPUSCH, John and John Gay.
  Beggar's Opera.

PERGOLESI, Giovanni Battista.
  *La Serva Padrona.***

PFITZNER, Hans.
  Palestrina.

PONCHIELLI, Amilcare.
  La Gioconda.

PROKOFIEV, Serge.
  Cinderella (Ballet).* *The Flaming Angel. The Love for
  3 Oranges. War and Peace.**

PUCCINI, Giacomo.
   *La Boheme.*** *Madama Butterfly.*** *Manon Lescaut.***
   *Tosca.*** *Il Trittico.* *Turandot.**

PURCELL, Henry.
   *Dido and Aeneas.*** *Fairy Queen.* *King Arthur.*

RAMEAU, Jean-Philippe.
   *Castor et Pollux.** *Hippolyte et Aricie.*

RAVEL, Maurice.
   Daphnis et Chloe (Ballet).*** *Enfant et les Sortileges.*
   L"Heure Espagnole.

RIMSKY-KORSAKOV, Nikolai.
   *Legend of Tsar Sultan.** *Sadko.* *The Tsar's Bride.*

ROSSINI, Gioacchino.
   *Il Barbiere di Siviglia.*** *La Cenerentola.* *Guillaume*
   *Tell.** *Semiramide.*

SAINT-SAENS, Camille.
   Samson et Dalila.

SCHOENBERG, Arnold.
   Moses and Aaron (Oratorio).*

SHOSTAKOVICH, Dmitri.
   Lady Macbeth of Mzensk.

SPONTINI, Gasparo.
   La Vestale.

STRAUSS, Johann.
   *Die Fledermaus.**

STRAUSS, Richard.
   Arabella. *Ariadne auf Naxos.** *Elektra.** *Die Frau ohne*
   Schatten. *Der Rosenkavakier.*** *Salome.***

STRAVINSKY, Igor.
   The Firebird (Ballet).*** *Les Noces* (Ballet-Cantata).*
   Oedipus Rex. *Petrouchka* (Ballet).*** *Pulcinella* (Ballet).
   *The Rake's Progress.** *Le Rossignol* (Ballet). *Le Sacre*
   du Printemps (Ballet).**

TCHAIKOVSKY, Peter.
   Eugene Onegin. *The Nutcracker* (Ballet).*** *Pique-Dame.*
   Sleeping Beauty (Ballet).*** *Swan Lake* (Ballet).***

TELEMANN, Georg Philipp.
   Der Tag des Gerichts (Oratorio).

THOMAS, Ambroise.
   Mignon.

TIPPETT, Michael.
  A Midsummer Marriage.

VERDI, Giuseppe.
  *Aida.*** *Un Ballo in Maschera.** *Don Carlos. Falstaff.**
  *La Forza del Destino. Macbeth. Othello.** *Rigoletto.***
  *La Traviata.*** *Il Trovatore.***

WAGNER, Richard.
  *Der Fliegende Hollander.** *Die Gotterdammerung.**
  *Lohengrin.** *Die Meistersinger.*** *Parsifal.*** *Das*
  *Rheingold.** *Siegfried.** *Tannhauser.** *Tristan und*
  *Isolde. Die Walkure.**

WEBER, Carl Maria Von.
  *Der Freischutz.**

WEILL, Kurt.
  Aufstieg und Fall der Stadt Mahagonny. Die
  *Dreigroschenoper.***

POPULAR

ALPERT, Herb, and the Tijuana Brass. *Going Places.* A&M.
  Whipped Cream and Other Delights. A&M.*

ANDREWS SISTERS. *Best.* MCA.*

BENNETT, Tony. *I Left My Heart in San Francisco/Hits Today.*
  2-Columbia.

CAMPBELL, Glen. *Best.* Capitol.*

CANNON, Ace. *Peace in the Valley.* Hi.

CONIFF, Ray. *After the Lovin'.* Columbia.

CROSBY, Bing and Fred Astaire. *A Couple of Song and Dance Men.*
  United Artists.

FAITH, Percy. *Great Moments of Percy Faith.* 2-Columbia.

FERRANTE AND TEICHER. *Piano Portraits.* United Artists.

HUMPERDINCK, Engelbert. *After the Lovin'.* Epic.**

JONES, Tom. *Greatest Hits.* Parrot.**

MANILOW, Barry. *II.* Bell.**

MANTOVANI. *Romantic Hits.* 2-London.

MARTINO, Al. *Best.* Capitol.

MATHIS, Johnny. *Greatest Hits.* Columbia.*

MIDLER, Bette. *Divine Miss M.* Atlantic.

MILLS BROTHERS. *Best.* Paramount.

RANDOLPH, Boots. *Sax Appeal*. Monument.

SINATRA, Frank. *No One Cares*. Capitol.**

STREISAND, Barbra. *The Way We Were*. Columbia.**

WELK, Lawrence. *Best of Lawrence Welk*. Ranwood.*

WILLIAMS, Andy. *Moon River/Days of Wine and Roses*. 2-Columbia.

ROCK, SOUL

AEROSMITH. *Get Your Wings*. Columbia.**

AKKERMAN, Jan. *Tabernakel*. Atco.

ALICE COOPER. *School's Out*. Warner Brothers.**

ALLMAN BROTHERS BAND. *Brothers and Sisters*. Capricorn. *Eat A Peach*. 2-Capricorn.* *Live at the Fillmore*. 2-Capricorn.*

ALLMAN, Greg. *Laid Back*. Capricorn.

AMERICA. *Greatest Hits*. Warner Brothers.**

AMON DUUL II. *Dance of the Lemmings*. 2-United Artists.

ANIMALS. *Animal Tracks*. MGM. *Greatest Hits*. MGM.**

ANKA, Paul. *Anka Gold--28 Original Hits*. 2-Sire.**

ARS NOVA. *Sunshine and Shadows*. Atlantic.

BABE RUTH. *First Base*. Harvest.

BACHMAN-TURNER OVERDRIVE. *Not Fragile*. Mercury.**

BADFINGER. *No Dice*. Apple. *Wish You Were Here*. Warner Brothers.*

BAND. *The Band*. Capitol.* *Moondog Matinee*. Capitol. *Music From Big Pink*. Capitol.* *Rock of Ages*. 2-Capitol. *Stage Fright*. Capitol.

BAY CITY ROLLERS. *Rock and Roll Love Letter*. Arista.**

BEACH BOYS. *All Summer Long*. Capitol. *Endless Summer*. 2-Capitol.** *Holland*. Brother.* *Pet Sounds*. Capitol.* *Smiley Smile*. Brother. *Surfin' U.S.A.* Capitol. *Surf's Up*. Brother.

BEATLES. *Abbey Road*. Apple.* *The Beatles*. 2-Apple.* *Hard Day's Night*. United Artists. *Help*. Capitol. *Introducing the Beatles*. Vee Jay. *Magical Mystery Tour*. Capitol. *Meet the Beatles*. Capitol. *1967-1970*. 2-Apple.** *1962-1966*. 2-Apple.** *Revolver*. Capitol.* *Rubber Soul*. Capitol.* *Sargeant Pepper's Lonely Hearts Club Band*. Capitol.* *Volume 2*. Capitol. *Yesterday and Today*. Capitol.

BEE GEES. *First.* Atco. *Gold, Volume 1.* RSO.** *Main Course.* RSO.* *Odessa.* 2-Atco.

BERRY, Chuck. *Golden Decade.* Chess.**

BLACK SABBATH. *Paranoid.* Warner Brothers.

BLIND FAITH. *Blind Faith.* Atco.

BLUE OYSTER CULT. *Blue Oyster Cult.* Columbia.* *Secret Treaties.* Columbia. *Tyranny and Mutation.* Columbia.

BLUNSTONE, Colin. *Ennismore.* Epic.

BOONE, Pat. *Greatest Hits.* 2-Paramount.**

BOWIE, David. *Alladin Sane.* RCA. *Low.* RCA. *The Rise and Fall of Ziggy Stardust and the Spiders from Mars.* RCA.* *Young Americans.* RCA.**

BROWNE, Jackson. *For Everyman.* Asylum.*

BROWNSVILLE STATION. *School Punks.* Big Tree.

BUFFALO SPRINGFIELD. *Again.* Atco.* *Last Time Around.* Atco.

BYRDS. *Best.* Columbia.** *Mr. Tambourine Man.* Columbia. *The Notorious Byrd Brothers.* Columbia. *Sweetheart of the Rodeo.* Columbia.

CAN. *Future Days.* United Artists.

CANNED HEAT. *Living the Blues.* 2-Liberty.

CARMEN, Eric. *Eric Carmen.* Arista.*

CHICAGO. *Chicago Transit Authority.* 2-Columbia. *Chicago II.* 2-Columbia.**

CLAPTON, Eric. *Best.* 2-Polydor.* *E.C. Was Here.* RSO.

CLARK, Dick. *20 Years of Rock 'N' Roll.* 2-Buddah.**

CLIMAX BLUES BAND. *Rich Man.* Sire. *Sense of Direction.* Sire.*

COASTERS. *Greatest Hits.* Atlantic.**

COCHRAN, Eddie. *Legendary Masters.* 2-United Artists.*

COODER, Ry. *Paradise and Lunch.* Reprise.*

COUNTRY JOE AND THE FISH. *I-Feel-Like-I'm-Fixin'-To-Die-Rag.* Vanguard.

CRAZY HORSE. *Crazy Horse.* Reprise.

CREAM. *Heavy Cream.* 2-Polydor.**

CREEDENCE CLEARWATER REVIVAL. *Bayou Country.* Fantasy. *Gold.* Fantasy.** *Pendulum.* Fantasy. *Willie and the Poor Boys.* Fantasy.*

CROCE, Jim. *Photographs and Memories (Greatest Hits)*. ABC.**

CROSBY, STILLS AND NASH. *Crosby, Stills and Nash*. Atlantic.**

CROWBAR. *Bad Manors*. Paramount.

DARIN, Bobby. *Greatest Hits*. Atco.*

DEEP PURPLE. *Book of Taliesyn*. Tetragrammaton. *In Rock*. Warner Brothers.* *Machine Head*. Warner Brothers. *Made in Japan*. 2-Warner Brothers.* *Purple Passages*. 2-Warner Brothers.**

DENVER, John. *Greatest Hits*. RCA.**

DEREK AND THE DOMINOS. *Layla*. 2-Atco.**

DIAMOND, Neil. *Double Gold*. Bang. *His 12 Greatest Hits*. MCA.**

DION. *Greatest Hits*. Columbia.*

DOMINO, Fats. *Legendary Masters*. 2-United Artists.**

DONOVAN. *Sunshine Superman*. Epic.

DOOBIE BROTHERS. *The Captain and Me*. Warner Brothers.*

DOORS. *The Doors*. Elektra. *Strange Days*. Elektra.*

DRIFTERS. *Greatest Hits*. Atlantic.**

DUCK'S DELUXE. *Duck's Deluxe*. RCA.

DYLAN, Bob. *Another Side of Bob Dylan*. Columbia.* *Before the Flood*. 2-Asylum. *Blonde on Blonde*. 2-Columbia.* *Blood on the Tracks*. Columbia.** *Freewheelin'*. Columbia. *Highway 61*. Columbia.* *John Wesley Harding*. Columbia.* *Nashville Skyline*. Columbia.

EAGLES. *The Eagles*. Asylum. *One of These Nights*. Asylum.**

EARTH, WIND AND FIRE. *Open Our Eyes*. Columbia. *That's the Way of the World*. Columbia.**

ELECTRIC LIGHT ORCHESTRA. *On the Third Day*. United Artists.

EMERSON, LAKE AND PALMER. *Trilogy*. Cotillion.*

ENO. *Another Green World*. Island.

EVERLY BROTHERS. *Greatest Hits*. 2-Barnaby.**

FABIAN. *16 Greatest Hits*. ABC.

FACES. *First Step*. Warner Brothers.

FAIRPORT CONVENTION. *Full House*. A&M. *Liege and Lief*. A&M.*

FLASH CADILLAC AND THE CONTINENTAL KIDS. *Flash Cadillac and the Continental Kids*. Epic.*

FLEETWOOD MAC. *Black Magic Woman*. 2-Epic. *Fleetwood Mac*.
Reprise.** *Kiln House*. Reprise.* *Then Play On*. Reprise.

FLEETWOODS. *Very Best of the Fleetwoods*. United Artists.

FLYING BURRITO BROTHERS. *The Flying Burrito Brothers*. A&M.
Gilded Palace of Sin. A&M.

FOCUS. *Focus 3*. 2-Sire.* *Hamburger Concerto*. Sire.

FOGHAT. *Fool for the City*. Bearsville.**

FOUR TOPS. *Anthology*. 3-Motown.**

FRAMPTON, Peter. *Frampton Comes Alive*. 2-A&M.**

FRANKLIN, Aretha. *Amazing Grace*. 2-Atlantic.* *Greatest
Hits*. Atlantic.**

FREE. *Fire and Water*. A&M.* *Highway*. A&M.

FUNKADELIC. *Cosmic Slop*. Westbound.* *Maggot Brain*.
Westbound.

GALLAGHER, Rory. *Blueprint*. Polydor.

GAYE, Marvin. *Anthology*. 3-Motown.** *What's Goin' On*.
Tamla.*

GAYNOR, Gloria. *Never Can Say Goodbye*. MGM.

GEILS BAND, J. *Nightmares...and Other Tales from the Vinyl
Jungle*. Atlantic.

GENESIS. *Selling England By the Pound*. Charisma.*

GENTLE GIANT. *Free Hand*. Capitol.* *Octopus*. Columbia.

GRAND FUNK RAILROAD. *Closer to Home*. Capitol. *We're An
American Band*. Capitol.**

GRATEFUL DEAD. *Anthem of the Sun*. Warner Brothers. *Blues
for Allah*. Grateful Dead. *Live/Dead*. 2-Warner Brothers.**
Workingman's Dead. Warner Brothers.*

GREEN, Al. *Call Me*. Hi.*

GROUNDHOGS. *Hogwash*. United Artists.

GUESS WHO. *Best*. RCA.*

GUTHRIE, Arlo. *Alice's Restaurant*. Reprise.**

HALEY, Bill, and the Comets. *Rock 'N' Roll*. Pickwick.**

HARRIS, Emmylou. *Pieces of the Sky*. Reprise.

HARRISON, George. *All Things Must Pass*. 3-Apple.*

HAWKWIND. *In the Hall of the Mountain Grill*. United Artists.

HAYES, Isaac. *Hot Buttered Soul*. Enterprise.*

HENDRIX, Jimi. *Are You Experienced?* Reprise.* *Cry of Love*. Reprise. *Electric Ladyland*. 2-Reprise.**

HICKS, Dan, and the Hot Licks. *Last Train to Hicksville*. Blue Thumb.

HOLLIES. *Beat Group*. Imperial. *Greatest Hits*. Epic.** *Out On the Road*. Hansa (Import). *Stop, Stop, Stop*. Imperial.

HOLLY, Buddy. *Greatest Hits*. Epic.**

HUMBLE PIE. *Rockin' the Fillmore*. 2-A&M. *Smokin'*. A&M.*

ISLEY BROTHERS. *The Heat Is On*. T-Neck. *Very Best*. United Artists.*

IT'S A BEAUTIFUL DAY. *It's A Beautiful Day*. Columbia.*

JACKSON, Millie. *Still Caught Up*. Spring.*

JACKSON 5. *Anthology*. 3-Motown.

JAMES, Tommy. *Hanky Panky*. Roulette.

JAMES GANG. *16 Greatest Hits*. 2-ABC.

JAN AND DEAN. *Legendary Masters*. 2-United Artists.**

JEFFERSON AIRPLANE. *After Bathing at Baxter's*. RCA.** *Surrealistic Pillow*. RCA.

JEFFERSON STARSHIP. *Red Octopus*. Grunt.**

JETHRO TULL. *Aqualung*. Reprise. *Stand Up*. Reprise.*

JOEL, Billy. *Piano Man*. Columbia.

JOHN, Elton. *Goodbye Yellow Brick Road*. 2-MCA.* *Greatest Hits*. MCA.**

JOPLIN, Janis. *Cheap Thrills* (with Big Brother and the Holding Company). Columbia.** *Pearl*. Columbia.

KALEIDOSCOPE. *A Beacon From Mars*. Epic. *Side Trips*. Epic.

KING, Carole. *Tapestry*. Ode.**

KING CRIMSON. *In the Court of the Crimson King*. Atlantic.* *Larks Tongues in Aspic*. Atlantic.

KINGSMEN. *Volume I*. Wand.

KINKS. *Arthur*. Reprise. *Face to Face*. Reprise. *Greatest Hits*. Reprise.** *Muswell Hillbillies*. RCA.*

KNIGHT, Gladys, and the Pips. *Anthology*. 2-Motown.

KOOL AND THE GANG. *Spirit of the Boogie*. De-Lite.

KOTTKE, Leo. *Greenhouse*. Capitol.

KRAFTWERK. *Autobahn*. Vertigo.

LABELLE. *Nightbirds*. Epic.

LED ZEPPELIN. *Four*. Atlantic.** *Houses of the Holy*. Atlantic. *Physical Graffiti*. 2-Swan Song.

LEE, Brenda. *The Brenda Lee Story*. 2-MCA.**

LENNON, John. *Imagine*. Apple.* *Rock 'N' Roll*. Apple.*

LEWIS, Jerry Lee. *Greatest Hits*. Sun.**

LIGHTFOOT, Gordon. *Sundown*. Reprise.

LITTLE ANTHONY AND THE IMPERIALS. *Very Best*. United Artists.

LITTLE FEAT. *Feats Don't Fail Me Now*. Warner Brothers.

LITTLE RICHARD. *Big Hits*. GNP.**

LOGGINS AND MESSINA. *Sittin' In*. Columbia. *Full Sail*. Columbia.*

LOVE. *Four Sail*. Elektra. *Out Here*. 2-Blue Thumb.

LOVIN' SPOONFUL. *Do You Believe in Magic?* Kama Sutra. *Greatest Hits*. Kama Sutra.

LYNYRD SKYNYRD. *Pronounced Lynyrd Skynyrd*. MCA.* *Second Helping*. MCA.

MCCARTNEY, Paul. *Ram*. Apple.

MCLEAN, Don. *Don McLean*. United Artists.

MAHAVISHNU ORCHESTRA. *Birds of Fire*. Columbia.

MAMAS AND THE PAPAS. *20 Golden Hits*. Dunhill.**

MANASSAS. *Manassas*. 2-Atco.

MARSHALL TUCKER BAND. *Marshall Tucker Band*. Capricorn.*

MATTHEWS, Ian. *Valley Hi*. Elektra.

MAYALL, John. *Best*. Polydor.*

MELVIN, Harold, and the Blue Notes. *To Be True*. Philadelphia International.

METERS. *Rejuvenation*. Reprise.*

MFSB. *MFSB*. Philadelphia International.

MILLER, Steve, Band. *Fly Like an Eagle*. Capitol.** *Sailor*. Capitol.* *Your Saving Grace*. Capitol.

MITCHELL, Joni. *Court and Spark*. Elektra/Asylum.**

MOBY GRAPE. *Moby Grape*. Columbia. *69*. Columbia. *Wow/Grape Jam*. 2-Columbia.

MONKEES. *Greatest Hits*. Arista.** *Headquarters*. Colgems.

MOODY BLUES. *Days of Future Passed*. Deram.** *In Search of the Lost Chord*. Deram. *On the Threshold of A Dream*. Deram.**

MORRISON, Van. *Astral Weeks*. Warner Brothers. *Moondance*. Warner Brothers.** *Them, Featuring Van Morrison*. Parrot.

MOTHERS OF INVENTION (featuring Frank Zappa). *Freak Out*. Verve. *We're Only in it for the Money*. Verve.*

MOTT THE HOOPLE. *All the Young Dudes*. Columbia.*

MOVE. *Split Ends*. United Artists.

NASH, Johnny. *I Can See Clearly Now*. Epic.

NEKTAR. *Remember the Future*. Passport.

NELSON, Rick. *Legendary Masters*. 2-United Artists.**

NEWMAN, Randy. *Good Old Boys*. Reprise.*

NEWTON-JOHN, Olivia. *If You Love Me, Let Me Know*. MCA.**

NEW YORK DOLLS. *New York Dolls*. Mercury.*

NILSSON. *Harry*. RCA. *Nilsson Schmilsson*. RCA.*

NITTY GRITTY DIRT BAND. *Uncle Charlie and His Dog Teddy*. Liberty. *Will the Circle Be Unbroken*. 3-United Artists.*

OHIO PLAYERS. *Honey*. Mercury.*

O'JAYS. *Greatest Hits*. United Artists.*

OLDFIELD, Mike. *Tubular Bells*. Virgin.**

ORBISON, Roy. *Greatest Hits*. Monument.**

OSIBISA. *Woyaya*. MCA.*

PARSONS, Gram. *Grievous Angel*. Reprise.

PAUL, Billy. *War of the Gods*. Philadelphia International.

PEARLS BEFORE SWINE. *Balaklava*. ESP. *These Things Too*. Reprise.*

PICKETT, Bobby "Boris." *Monster Mash*. Parrot.

PINK FAIRIES. *What A Bunch of Sweeties*. Polydor (Import).

PINK FLOYD. *Atom Heart Mother*. Harvest. *Dark Side of the Moon*. Harvest.** *Obscured By Clouds*. Harvest. *Ummagumma*. 2-Harvest.

PITNEY, Gene. *Big 16*. Musicor.*

POCO. *Crazy Eyes*. Epic. *Picking Up the Pieces*. Epic. *Poco*. Epic.

PRESLEY, Elvis. *Blue Hawaii*. RCA. *Fifty Golden Hits*. 4-RCA.** *The Sun Collection*. RCA.**

PRETTY THINGS. *Solk Torpedo*. Swan Song.

PROCOL HARUM. *Procol Harum*. Deram.** *A Salty Dog*. A&M.* *Shine On Brightly*. A&M.

QUICKSILVER MESSENGER SERVICE. *Happy Trails*. Capitol.* *Quicksilver Messenger Service*. Capitol.

RASCALS. *Once Upon A Dream*. Atlantic. *Time/Peace (Greatest Hits)*. Atlantic.**

RASPBERRIES. *Side 3*. Capitol. *Starting Over*. Capitol.*

REED, Lou. *Lou Reed*. RCA. *Rock 'N' Roll Animal*. RCA.**

REEVES, Martha, and the Vandellas. *Anthology*. 2-Motown.**

RENAISSANCE. *Scheherazade*. Sire.

REVERE, Paul, and the Raiders. *Steppin' Out*. Columbia.

RHINOCEROS. *Better Days*. Elektra. *Satin Chickens*. Elektra.

RIGHTEOUS BROTHERS. *Best*. Verve.*

RIVERS, Johnny. *Live at the Whiskey-A-Go-Go*. Imperial. *Very Best*. United Artists.**

ROBINSON, Smokey, and the Miracles. *Anthology*. 3-Motown.**

ROLLING STONES. *Beggar's Banquet*. London.* *Between the Buttons*. London. *Exile on Main Street*. 2-Rolling Stones.** *Get Yer Ya-Yas Out*. London. *Let It Bleed*. London. *Now*. London.* *Rolling Stones*. London. *Sticky Fingers*. Rolling Stones. *Their Satanic Majesties Request*. London.*

RONSTADT, Linda. *Heart Like A Wheel*. Capitol.**

ROSS, Diana, and the Supremes. *Anthology*. 3-Motown.**

ROXY MUSIC. *For Your Pleasure*. Warner Brothers. *Stranded*. Atco.*

RUNDGREN, Todd. *Something/Anything*. 2-Bearsville.** *Todd*. 2-Bearsville. *A Wizard, A True Star*. Bearsville.

SAM THE SHAM AND THE PHAROHS. *On Tour*. MGM.

SANTANA. *Abraxas*. Columbia.** *Barboletta*. Columbia. *Caravanserai*. Columbia. *Santana*. Columbia.*

SEGER, Bob. *Night Moves*. Capitol.

SHA NA NA. *Streets of New York*. Kama Sutra.*

SHANNON, Del. *The Vintage Years*. 2-Sire.

SHIRELLES. *Very Best*. United Artists.*

SIMON, Carly. *No Secrets*. Elektra.

SIR DOUGLAS BAND. *Texas Tornado*. Atlantic.

SNOW, Phoebe. *Phoebe Snow*. Shelter.*

SOFT MACHINE. *Six*. 2-Columbia.

SONNY AND CHER. *Greatest Hits*. MCA.**

SPARKS. *Kimono My House*. Island.

SPOOKY TOOTH. *Spooky Two*. A&M.

SPRINGSTEEN, Bruce. *Born to Run*. Columbia.** *The Wild, the Innocent, and the E Street Shuffle*. Columbia.

STEELEYE SPAN. *Parcel of Rogues*. Chrysalis.

STEELY DAN. *Countdown to Ecstasy*. ABC.* *Pretzel Logic*. ABC.

STEPPENWOLF. *At Your Birthday Party*. Dunhill. *The Second*. Dunhill.

STOOGES (featuring Iggy Pop). *Raw Power*. Columbia.

STORIES. *About Us*. Buddah.

TALKING HEADS. *Talking Heads: '77*. Sire.

TANGERINE DREAM. *Phaedra*. Virgin.

TEMPTATIONS. *Anthology*. 3-Motown.**

10CC. *Sheet Music*. UK.

THREE DOG NIGHT. *Joy to the World (Greatest Hits)*. Dunhill.

TOWER OF POWER. *Urban Renewal*. Warner Brothers.

TRAPEZE. *Hot Wire*. Warner Brothers.

TROWER, Robin. *Bridge of Sighs*. Chrysalis.*

TURNER, Ike and Tina. *Best*. Blue Thumb.

TYRANNOSAURUS REX. *Unicorn*. Blue Thumb.

UFO. *No Heavy Petting*. Chrysalis. *Phenomenon*. Chrysalis.*

URIAH HEEP. *Magician's Birthday*. Mercury.

VARIOUS ARTISTS. *History of British Rock, Volume 1*. 2-Sire.** *History of British Rock, Volume 2*. 2-Sire.** *Original Early Top 40 Hits*. 2-Paramount.*

VELVET UNDERGROUND. *1969 Live*. 2-Mercury.

VENTURES. *Very Best*. United Artists.**

WAINRIGHT, Loudon, III. *Album III*. Columbia.

WAITS, Tom. *The Heart of Saturday*. Elektra/Asylum.

WALKER, Junior, and the All Stars. *Anthology*. 2-Motown.

WALSH, Joe. *The Smoker You Drink, the Player You Get*. Dunhill.

WAR. *The World Is A Ghetto*. United Artists.*

WARWICKE, Dionne. *Very Best*. United Artists.*

WET WILLIE. *Keep On Smilin'*. Capricorn.

WHO. *Live at Leeds*. MCA.** *My Generation*. Decca. *Quadraphrenia*. 2-MCA. *Tommy*. 2-Decca.** *Who's Next*. MCA.**

WILSON, Jackie. *Greatest Hits*. Brunswick.

WINGS (featuring Paul McCartney). *Band on the Run*. Apple.** *Wings Over America*. 3-Capitol.

WINTER, Johnny. *Captured Live*. Columbia.* *Second Winter*. 2-Columbia.

WONDER, Stevie. *Fulfillingness First Finale*. Tamla.* *Greatest Hits*. Tamla.** *Innervisions*. Tamla.** *Songs in the Key of Life*. 2-Tamla.** *Talking Book*. Tamla.

WOOD, Roy. *Boulders*. United Artists.

YARDBIRDS. *Greatest Hits*. Epic.* *Over Under Sideways Down*. Epic.

YES. *Close to the Edge*. Atlantic.** *Fragile*. Atlantic. *Yessongs*. 3-Atlantic.*

YOUNG, Neil. *After the Goldrush*. Reprise.** *Everybody Knows This Is Nowhere*. Reprise.** *Harvest*. Reprise.* *Neil Young*. Reprise. *Time Fades Away*. Reprise. *Zuma*. Reprise.

ZZ TOP. *Tres Hombres*. London.*

Appendix 1

BIBLIOGRAPHY

The books included in this listing were chosen with regard to
their applicability to the selection of sound recordings. In
other words, those works have been included which provide the
reader with the type of knowledge necessary to successfully
undertake the responsibilities involved in record and tape
selection in the various musical fields. Books within the
area of librarianship that are concerned with inculcating
selection principles in the audiovisual sector have been omit-
ted because, in most cases, they have not provided any grounding
in music appreciation.

The author has attempted to include only those books in
print at some point between mid-1972 and mid-1977. (Bowker's
Books in Print was employed as a verification tool in this
process.) The listing was also compiled with a preference for
works bearing a relatively recent date of publication. This
was particularly the case with respect to the popular music
genres, due to the fact that their continual evolution would
render a published work outdated almost as soon as it appeared

on the market.   The subject breakdowns utilized here mirror the
Library of Congress headings, which have been appropriated by
libraries and reference sources throughout the country.

JAZZ MUSIC

Balliett, Whitney. *Dinosaurs in the Morning: Forty-One Pieces
    on Jazz.* Reprint ed. Scholarly Publications, 1962.

Blesh, Rudi and Janis, Harriet. *They All Played Ragtime.*
    Rev. ed. Quick Fox, n.d.

Condon, Eddie. *We Called It Music: A Generation of Jazz.*
    Greenwood, 1947.

Dankworth, Avril. *Jazz: An Introduction to Its Musical Basis.*
    Oxford University Press, 1968.

DeToledano, Ralph. *Frontiers of Jazz.* 2d ed. Ungar, 1962.

Dexter, Dave. *Jazz Story: From the Nineties to the Sixties.*
    Prentice-Hall, 1964.

Feather, Leonard. *Book of Jazz: From Then till Now.* Rev. ed.
    Horizon, n.d.

Feather, Leonard. *From Satchmo to Miles.* Stein & Day, 1972.

Hodeir, Andre. *Jazz: Its Evolution and Essence.* Noakes, David,
    tr. Grove, 1961.

Jones, LeRoi. *Black Music.* Morrow, 1967.

Keil, Charles. *Urban Blues.* University of Chicago Press, 1966.

Longstreet, Stephen. *Real Jazz, Old and New.* Greenwood, 1956.

McCarthy, Albert, et al. *Jazz on Record: The First Fifty Years,
    1917 to 1967.* Quick Fox, 1969.

Mehegan, John. *Jazz Improvisation.* 4 Vols. Including: Vol. 1,
    Tonal and Rhythmic Principles; Vol. 2, *Jazz Rhythm and Impro-
    vised Line*; Vol. 3, *Swing and Early Progressive Styles*; Vol. 4,
    Contemporary Piano Styles. Simon and Schuster, 1968.

Oliver, Paul. *Aspects of the Blues Tradition.* Quick Fox, 1970.

Schuller, Gunther. *Early Jazz: Its Roots and Musical Develop-
    ment.* Oxford University Press, 1968.

Stearns, Marshall. *Story of Jazz.* Oxford University Press,
    1956.

Ulanov, Barry. *A History of Jazz in America.* Reprint of 1955 ed. DaCapo, 1972.

Williams, Martin. *Jazz Tradition.* Oxford University Press, 1970.

MUSIC--HISTORY AND CRITICISM

Abraham, Gerald, ed. *The History of Music in Sound, Vols. 1-10.* Including: Vol. 1, *Ancient and Oriental Music*; Vol. 2, *Early Medieval Music up to 1300*; Vol. 3, *Ars Nova and the Renaissance, c. 1300-1540*; Vol. 4, *The Age of Humanism, 1540-1630*; Vol. 5, *Opera and Church Music, 1630-1750*; Vol. 6, *The Growth of Instrumental Music, 1630-1750*; Vol. 7, *Symphonic Outlook, 1750-90*; Vol. 8, *The Age of Beethoven, 1790-1830*; Vol. 9, *Romanticism, 1830-90*; Vol. 10, *Modern Music, 1890-1950.* Oxford University Press, 1953-59.

Apel, Willi. *History of Keyboard Music Before 1700.* Tischler, Hans, tr. Indiana University Press, 1972.

Bekker, Paul. *Story of Music: An Historical Sketch of the Changes in Musical Form.* Reprint of 1927 ed. A.M.S. Press, 1970.

Bernier, Rosamond, ed. *Illustrated History of Music.* Reynal, 1959.

Borroff, Edith. *Music in Europe and the United States: A History.* Prentice-Hall, 1971.

Boyden, David D. *Introduction to Music.* 2d ed., rev. Knopf, 1970.

Brockway, Wallace and Weinstock, Herbert. *Men of Music.* Simon and Schuster, 1950.

Burney, Charles. *General History of Music.* 2 Vols. Dover, 1935.

Busby, Thomas. *General History of Music from the Earliest Times.* 2 Vols. DaCapo, 1968.

Cannon, Beekman C., et al. *Art of Music.* Crowell, 1960.

Chailley, Jacques. *Forty Thousand Years of Music.* Meyers, R., tr. Farrar, Straus & Giroux, 1965.

Colles, H. C. *The Growth of Music: A Study in Musical History.* 3 Parts. Rev. by Eric Blom. Part 1, *From the Troubadors to J. S. Bach.* 3d ed. Part 2, *The Age of the Sonata from C. P. E. Bach to Beethoven.* 2d ed. Part 3, *The Ideals of the Nineteenth Century; The Twentieth Century.* 2d ed. Oxford University Press, 1956.

Cooke, J. F. *Standard History of Music.* Gordon, n.d.

Davison, Archibald and Apel, Willi, eds. *Historical Anthology of Music.* 2 Vols. Vol. 1, *Oriental, Medieval, and Renaissance Music.* Rev. ed. 1949. Vol. 2, *Baroque, Rococo, and Pre-Classical Music.* Harvard University Press, 1950.

Demuth, Norman. *An Anthology of Musical Criticism.* Reprint of 1947 ed. Greenwood, 1972.

Einstein, Alfred. *Short History of Music.* Knopf, 1954.

Elson, Louis. *Curiosities of Music.* Gordon, n.d.

Elson, Louis. *History of American Music.* Reprint. Franklin, 1971.

Ewen, David, ed. *From Bach to Stravinsky: The History of Music by Its Foremost Critics.* Reprint of 1933 ed. Greenwood, 1968.

Fellowes, E. H., et al. *Heritage of Music, Vol. 2.* Facsimile ed. Foss, Hubert J., ed. Reprint of 1934 ed. Books for Libraries, n.d.

Gelatt, Roland. *Music Makers.* Reprint of 1953 ed. Plenum, 1972.

Gerboth, Walter, et al., eds. *Introduction to Music: Selected Readings.* Rev. ed. Norton, 1969.

Gillespie, John. *Five Centuries of Keyboard Music.* Dover, 1972.

Graf, Max. *Modern Music: Composers and Music of Our Time.* Reprint of 1946 ed. Kennikat, 1969.

Gray, Cecil. *History of Music.* Barnes and Noble, 1968.

Grout, Donald J. *History of Western Music.* Norton, 1960.

Grunfeld, Frederick V. *Art and Times of the Guitar: From the Hittites to the Hippies.* Macmillan, 1969.

Harmen, Alec and Mellers, Wilfrid. *Man and His Music.* 2 Vols. Reprint. Scholarly Publications, 1962.

Hays, William. *Twentieth-Century Views of Music History.* Scribner, 1972.

Hindley, Geoffrey, ed. *Larousse Encyclopedia of Music.* World, 1971.

Hitchcock, H. Wiley. *Music in the United States: A Historical Introduction.* Prentice-Hall, 1969.

Howe, Granville. *A Hundred Years of Music in America.* Reprint. Finch, 1889.

Jacobs, Arthur. *A Short History of Western Music.* Penguin, 1972.

Jeppesen, Knud. *The Style of Palestrina and the Dissonance.* Peter Smith, n.d.

Kirby, F. E. *Short History of Keyboard Music.* Free Press, 1966.

Lang, Paul H., ed. *Music in Western Civilization.* Norton, 1941.

Lovelock, William. *Concise History of Music.* Ungar, 1962.

McKinney, Howard D. and Anderson, W. R. *Music in History, The Evolution of an Art.* 3d ed. Reinhold, 1966.

Miller, Hugh M. *History of Music.* New ed. Barnes and Noble, 1972.

Morgenstern, Sam, ed. *Composers on Music: An Anthology of Composers' Writings.* Hillary, 1958.

Nef, Karl. *Outline History of Music.* Rev. ed. Pfatteicher, Carl F., tr. Columbia University Press, 1957.

The Oxford History of Music. 8 Vols. 2d ed. Reprint. Scholarly Publications, 1929-38.

Parrish, Carl and Ohl, John F. *Masterpieces of Music Before 1750.* Norton, 1951.

Parry, Charles H. *Evolution of the Art of Music.* Colles, Henry C., ed. Greenwood, 1930.

Percival, Allen. *Teach Yourself History of Music.* Dover, n.d.

Peyser, Joan. *The New Music: The Sense Behind the Sound.* Dell, 1972.

Pichierri, Louis. *Music in New Hampshire, 1623-1800.* Columbia University Press, 1960.

Pruniers, Henry. *A New History of Music: The Middle Ages to Mozart.* Reprint. Scholarly Publications, 1943.

Robertson, Alec and Stevens, Denis, eds. *A History of Music.* 2 Vols. Vol. 1, *Ancient Form to Polyphony.* 1962. Vol. 2, *Renaissance and Baroque.* 1965. Barnes and Noble.

Rosen, Charles. *Classical Styles: Haydn, Mozart, Beethoven.* Viking, 1971.

Sainsbury, John F. *Dictionary of Musicians from the Earliest Time.* 2 Vols. 2d ed. DaCapo, 1969.

Saint-Saens, Camille. *Outspoken Essays on Music.* Facsimile ed. Rothwell, F., tr. Books for Libraries, 1922.

Scholes, Percy A. *The Listener's History of Music*. 3 Vols.
Including: Vol. 1, *To Beethoven*. 7th ed.; Vol. 2, *The
Romantic and Nationalist Schools of the Nineteenth Century*.
4th ed.; Vol. 3, *To the Composers of Today*. 5th ed. Oxford
University Press, 1954.

Scholes, Percy A. *Miniature History of Music for the General
Reader and the Student*. 4th ed. Oxford University Press,
1955.

Scott, Cyril. *Music, Its Secret Influence Throughout the Ages*.
Gordon, n.d.

Spaeth, Sigmund G. *Great Symphonies: How to Recognize and
Remember Them*. Rev. ed.; reprint of 1952 ed. Greenwood,
1972.

Stevenson, Ronald. *Western Music*. St. Martin, 1972.

Tovey, Donald F. *The Forms of Music*. Rev. ed. World, 1972.

Turner, Walter J. *Music: A Short History*. 2d ed. Scholarly
Publications, 1949.

Ulrich, Homer and Pisk, Paul A. *History of Music and Musical
Style*. Harcourt, Brace, 1963.

Vaughn Williams, Ralph. *National Music and Other Essays*.
Oxford University Press, n.d.

Weingartner, Felix. *The Symphony Since Beethoven*. Gordon,
n.d.

Westerby, Herbert. *History of Pianoforte Music*. Reprint of
1924 ed. DaCapo, 1970.

Westrup, J. A., et al., eds. *New Oxford History of Music*.
Oxford University Press, 1954-60.

Westrup, Jack. *Introduction to Musical History*. Hutchinson,
1963.

White, John J. *Music in Western Culture: A Short History*.
William C. Brown, 1972.

Wiora, Walter. *Four Ages of Music*. Norton, M. Herter, tr.
Norton, 1965.

Wold, Milo A. and Cykler, Edmund. *Introduction to Music and
Art in the Western World*. 4th ed. William C. Brown, 1972.

Wold, Milo A. and Cykler, Edmund. *Outline History of Music*.
2d ed. William C. Brown, 1973.

MUSIC--HISTORY AND CRITICISM--18TH CENTURY

Blume, Friedrich. *Renaissance and Baroque, A Comprehensive Survey*. Norton, M. Herter, tr. Norton, 1967.

Borroff, Edith. *Music of the Baroque*. William C. Brown, 1970.

Bukofzer, Manfred F. *Music in the Baroque Era*. Norton, 1947.

Harmen, Alec and Milner, Anthony. *Late Renaissance and Baroque Music*. Schocken, 1969.

Newman, William S. *Sonata in the Classical Era*. University of North Carolina Press, 1963.

Palisca, Claude V. *Baroque Music*. Prentice-Hall, 1968.

Pauly, Reinhard G. *Music in the Classical Period*. Prentice-Hall, 1965.

MUSIC--HISTORY AND CRITICISM--19TH CENTURY

Abraham, Gerald. *Slavonic and Romantic Music*. St. Martin, 1968.

Einstein, Alfred. *Music in the Romantic Era*. Norton, 1947.

Hughes, Gervase. *Sidelights on a Century of Music, 1825-1924*. St. Martin, 1970.

Klaus, Kenneth B. *Romantic Period in Music*. Allyn and Bacon, 1970.

Longyear, R. M. *Nineteenth Century Romanticism in Music*. Prentice-Hall, 1969.

Salazar, Adolfo. *Music in Our Time: Trends in Music Since the Romantic Era*. Pope, Isabel, tr. Greenwood, 1946.

MUSIC--HISTORY AND CRITICISM--20TH CENTURY

Austin, William. *Music in the Twentieth Century*. Norton, 1966.

Battcock, Gregory, ed. *New Music: A Critical Anthology*. Dutton, 1971.

Bauer, Marion and Payser, Ethel. *Twentieth Century Music*. Rev. ed. Putnam, 1947.

Boretz, Benjamin and Cone, Edward T., eds. *Perspectives on American Composers*. Norton, 1971.

Boulez, Pierre. *Boulez on Music Today*. Harvard University Press, 1970.

Cohn, Arthur. *Twentieth-Century Music in Western Europe*. Reprint. DaCapo, 1972.

Collaer, Paul. *History of Modern Music.* Abeles, Sally, tr.
Grosset and Dunlap, 1963.

Cope, David H. *New Directions in Music: 1950-1970.* William C.
Brown, 1970.

Copland, Aaron. *New Music: 1900-1960.* Rev. ed. Norton, 1968.

Davies, Laurence. *Paths to Modern Music.* Scribner, 1971.

Deri, Otto. *Exploring Twentieth-Century Music.* Holt, Rinehart
and Winston, 1968.

Ewen, David. *Twentieth Century Composers.* Facsimile ed. Books
for Libraries, 1937.

Ewen, David, ed. *New Book of Modern Composers.* Rev. ed.
Knopf, n.d.

Gray, Cecil. *Survey of Contemporary Music.* Books for Libraries,
1924.

Hansen, Peter S. *Introduction to Twentieth Century Music.* 3d
ed. Allyn and Bacon, 1971.

Hines, Robert S., ed. *Orchestral Composer's Point of View:
Essays on Twentieth Century Music by Those Who Wrote It.*
University of Oklahoma Press, 1970.

Lang, Paul H., ed. *Problems of Modern Music.* Norton, 1962.

Lang, Paul H. and Broder, Nathan, eds. *Contemporary Music in
Europe: A Comprehensive Survey.* Norton, 1967.

Leibowitz, Rene. *Schoenberg and His School: The Contemporary
Stage of the Language of Music.* Newlin, Dika, tr. Reprint
of 1949 ed. DaCapo, 1970.

Machlis, Joseph. *Introduction to Contemporary Music.* Norton,
1961.

Mellers, Wilfrid. *Romanticism and the Twentieth Century.*
Schocken, 1969.

Mitchell, Donald. *Language of Modern Music.* 3d ed. St. Martin,
1970.

Pleasants, Henry. *Agony of Modern Music.* Simon and Schuster,
1962.

Salzman, Eric. *Twentieth-Century Music: An Introduction.*
Prentice-Hall, 1967.

Schwartz, E. and Childs, B., eds. *Contemporary Composers on
Contemporary Music.* Holt, Rinehart and Winston, 1967.

Slonimsky, Nicholas. *Music Since 1900.* 4th ed. Scribner,
1971.

Stuckenschmidt, H. H. *Twentieth Century Music*. McGraw-Hill, 1969.

Thomson, Virgil. *American Music Since 1910*. Holt, Rinehart and Winston, 1971.

Wennerstrom, Mary H. *Anthology of Twentieth Century Music*. Appleton, 1969.

Yates, Peter. *Twentieth Century Music*. Funk and Wagnalls, n.d.

MUSIC, POPULAR

Brown, Len and Friedrich, Gary. *Do You Think You Know Rock 'n' Roll*. Tower, 1971.

Cohn, Nik. *Rock from the Beginning*. Stein and Day, 1969.

Eisen, Jonathan, ed. *Twenty-Minute Fandangoes and Forever Changes: A Rock Bazaar*. Random, 1971.

Gleason, Ralph. *Jefferson Airplane and the San Francisco Sound*. Ballantine, 1969.

Goldman, Albert. *Freakshow*. Atheneum, 1971.

Pulling, Christopher. *They Were Singing, and What They Sang About*. Reprint. Finch, 1952.

Sander, Ellen. *Trips: Rock Life in the Sixties*. Scribner, 1972.

Somma, Robert, ed. *No One Waved Goodbye: A Casualty Report on Rock and Roll*. Outerbridge, 1971.

Walley, David. *No Commercial Potential: The Saga of Frank Zappa and the Mothers of Invention*. Outerbridge, 1972.

MUSIC, POPULAR--DISCOGRAPHY

Armitage, Andrew B. and Tudor, Dean. *Annual Index to Popular Music Record Reviews, 1973*. Scarecrow, 1974.

Miles, Betty T., et al. *The Miles Chart Display, Vol. 1: Top 100, 1955-1970*. Rev. ed. Convex Industries, 1973.

Miles, Daniel J., et al. *The Miles Chart Display, Vol. 2: Top 100, 1971-1975*. Convex Industries, 1976.

Propes, Steve. *Golden Goodies: A Guide to 60's Record Collecting*. Chilton, 1974.

Propes, Steve. *Those Oldies But Goodies*. Macmillan, 1973.

Rust, Brian. *The American Dance Band Discography, 1917-1942*. Arlington House, 1976.

Rust, Brian and Debus, Allen. *The Complete Entertainment
    Discography: From Mid-1897 to 1942*. Arlington House, 1973.

Shaw, Arnold. *World of Soul: The Black Contribution to Pop
    Music*. Regnery, 1970.

Whitburn, Joel, ed. *Top Pop Records, 1955-1970*. Gale, 1972.

MUSIC, POPULAR--HISTORY AND CRITICISM

Belz, Carl. *The Story of Rock*. 2d ed. Oxford University
    Press, 1972.

Boeckman, Charles. *And the Beat Goes On: A History of Pop Music
    in America*. Luce, 1972.

Bruchac, Joseph. *The Poetry of Pop*. Dustbooks, 1973.

Burton, Jack. *Blue Book of Hollywood Musicals*. Century House,
    1952.

Burton, Jack. *Blue Book of Tin Pan Alley*. 2 Vols. Century
    House, n.d.

Chipman, Bruce L., ed. *Hardening Rock: An Organic Anthology
    of Rock 'n' Roll*. Little, Brown, 1972.

Davis, Clive and Willwerth, James. *Clive: Inside the Record
    Business*. Ballantine, 1976.

Denisoff, R. Serge and Peterson, Richard A., eds. *Sounds of
    Social Change: Studies in Popular Culture*. Rand, n.d.

Ewen, David. *All the Years of American Popular Music*.
    Prentice-Hall, 1976.

Ewen, David, ed. *Great Men of American Popular Song*. Rev. &
    enl. ed. Prentice-Hall, 1972.

Fong-Torres, Ben, ed. *The Rolling Stone Rock 'n' Roll Reader*.
    Bantam, 1974.

Freeman, Larry G. *Melodies Linger On*. Century House, 1951.

Garland, Phyl. *Sound of Soul*. Regnery, 1969.

Gentry, Linnell. *A History and Encyclopedia of Country, Western
    and Gospel Music*. Reprint. Scholarly Publications, 1961.

Gillett, Charlie. *Sound of the City: The Rise of Rock and
    Roll*. Dutton, 1970.

Goldberg, Isaac. *Tin Pan Alley*. Ungar, 1961.

Goldstein, Richard. *Goldstein's Greatest Hits: A Book Mostly
    About Rock 'N' Roll*. Prentice-Hall, 1970.

Goldstein, Stewart and Jacobson, Alan. *Oldies but Goodies*.
Mason Charter, 1976.

Goodman, Benny and Kolodin, Irving. *Kingdom of Swing*. Ungar,
n.d.

Grissim, John. *Country Music: White Man's Blues*. Paperback
Library, 1970.

Hemphill, Paul. *The Nashville Sound*. Ballantine, 1975.

Jahn, Mike. *Rock: From Elvis Presley to the Rolling Stones*.
Quadrangle, 1973.

Kinkle, Roger D. *The Complete Encyclopedia of Popular Music
and Jazz, 1900-1950*. 4 Vols. Arlington House, 1974.

Landau, Jon. *It's Too Late to Stop Now*. Quick Fox, n.d.

Laufe, Abe. *Broadway's Greatest Musical Hits*. 3d ed. Funk
and Wagnalls, 1973.

Lydon, Michael. *Rock Folk*. Dell, 1973.

Malone, Bill C. *Country Music, U.S.A.: A Fifty-Year History*.
University of Texas Press, 1969.

Marcus, Greil, ed. *Rock and Roll Will Stand*. Beacon Press,
1969.

Marcuse, Maxwell F. *Tin Pan Alley in Gaslight*. Century House,
n.d.

Mellers, Wilfred. *Twilight of the Gods: The Beatles in
Retrospect*. Viking, 1974.

Middleton, Richard. *Pop Music and the Blues: A Study of the
Relationship and Its Significance*. Humanities, 1972.

Nanry, Charles, ed. *American Music: From Storyville to Wood-
stock*. Transaction Books, 1975.

Oster, Harry. *Living Country Blues*. Gale, 1969.

Palmer, Tony. *All You Need Is Love: The Story of Popular Music*.
Grossman, 1976.

Pek, Ira, ed. *New Sound: Yes*. School Book Service, 1967.

Robinson, R., et al. *Rock Scene*. Pyramid, 1971.

Rolling Stone Editors. *Rolling Stone Interviews, No. 1*.
Warner, 1973.

Rolling Stone Editors. *Rolling Stone Interviews, No. 2*.
Warner, 1973.

Rooney, James. *Bossmen: Bill Monroe and Muddy Waters*. Dial,
1971.

Roxon, Lillian. *Rock Encyclopedia.* Grosset and Dunlap, 1971.

Schafer, William J. *Rock Music: Where It's Been, What It Means, Where It's Going.* Augsburg, 1972.

Shaw, Arnold. *Rock Revolution.* Rev. ed. Paperback Library, 1971.

Shaw, Arnold. *The Rockin' Fifties: The Decade That Transformed the Pop Music Scene.* Hawthorn, 1975.

Simon, George T. *Simon Says: The Sights and Sounds of the Swing Era, 1935-1955.* Arlington House, 1971.

Stambler, Irwin and Landon, Grelun. *Encyclopedia of Folk, Country and Western Music.* St. Martin, 1969.

Stambler, Irwin. *Encyclopedia of Pop, Rock and Soul.* St. Martin, 1976.

Stambler, Irwin and Landon, Grelun. *Golden Guitars: The Story of Country Music.* School Book Service, 1971.

Stormen, Win. *Jazz Piano: Dixieland Modern Jazz.* Arco, 1967.

Stormen, Win. *Jazz Piano: Ragtime to Rock Jazz.* Arco, 1975.

Swanwick, K. *Popular Music and the Teacher.* Pergamon, 1968.

Whitcomb, Ian. *After the Ball: Pop Music from Rag to Rock.* Simon and Schuster, 1974.

White, John I. *Git Along Little Dogies: Songs and Songmakers of the American West.* University of Illinois Press, 1975.

Wilder, Alec. *American Popular Song: The Great Innovators, 1900-1950.* Oxford University Press, 1972.

Williams, John R. *This Was Your Hit Parade: 1935-1950.* Courier-Gazette, 1973.

Williams, Paul. *Outlaw Blues: A Book of Rock Music.* Dutton, 1969.

Williams, Richard. *Out of His Head: The Sound of Phil Spector.* Dutton, 1972.

Whitmark, Isadore and Goldber, Isaac. *From Ragtime to Swingtime.* DaCapo, n.d.

OPERA

Austin, William W., ed. *New Looks at Italian Opera: Essays in Honor of Donald J. Grout.* Cornell University Press, 1968.

Berges, Ruth. *Backgrounds and Traditions of Opera.* A.S. Barnes, 1970.

Briggs, Thomas H. *Opera and Its Enjoyment*. Teachers' Collections, 1960.

Brockway, Wallace and Weinstock, Herbert. *World of Opera: The Story of Its Development and the Lore of Its Performance*. Pantheon, 1962.

Brody, Elaine. *Music in Opera: A Historical Anthology*. Prentice-Hall, 1970.

Coleman, Francis. *Bluff Your Way in Opera*. Crown, 1971.

Cooper, Martin. *Opera Comique*. Reprint. Scholarly Publications, 1949.

Dean, Winston. *Handel and the Opera Seria*. University of California Press, 1969.

Dent, Edward J. *Foundations of English Opera*. 2d ed. Reprint. DaCapo, 1967.

Graf, Herbert. *Opera for the People*. 2d ed. Reprint of 1951 ed. DaCapo, 1969.

Grout, Donald J. *Short History of Opera*. 2d ed. Columbia University Press, 1965.

Hartwood, Earl of, ed. *Kobbe's Complete Opera Book*. Putnam, 1972.

Howard, Patricia. *Gluck and the Birth of Modern Opera*. St. Martin, 1964.

Knapp, J. Merrill. *The Magic of Opera*. Harper and Row, 1973.

Lee, Ernest M. *Story of Opera*. Reprint of 1909 ed. Singing Tree, 1969.

Mackinlay, Sterling. *Origin and Development of Light Opera*. Blom, 1927.

Maynard, Olga. *Enjoying Opera*. Scribner, 1966.

Newman, Ernest. *Gluck and the Opera: A Study in Musical History*. International Publications Service, 1967.

Pauly, Reinhard G. *Music and the Theater: An Introduction to Opera*. Prentice-Hall, 1970.

Weisstein, U., ed. *Essence of Opera*. Free Press, 1964.

Woodhouse, Frederick. *Opera for Amateurs*. Dufour, 1951.

OPERA--HISTORY AND CRITICISM

Apthorp, W. F. *The Opera, Past and Present*. Gordon, n.d.

Jell, George. *Master Builders of Opera*. Books for Libraries, n.d.

Loewenberg, Alfred. *Annals of Opera, 1597-1940.* 2 Vols.
    Reprint of 1943 ed. Scholarly Publications, 1971.

Streatfield, Richard A. *The Opera: A Sketch of the Development
    of Opera.* Rev. ed. Reprint of 1932 ed. Greenwood, 1972.

OPERA--STORIES, PLOTS, ETC.

Morley, Alexander F. *The Harrap Opera Guide.* Dufour, 1971.

RATINGS OF RECORDED SOUND EQUIPMENT

While general guidelines in the selection of audio reproduction equipment have been outlined in Chapter 4, it is the purpose of this section to provide for librarians a basis of comparison between the leading products presently being manufactured. The ratings provided here were selected from a recent annual compilation of *Consumer Reports*, with the aim of concentrating on those areas of audio equipment most in demand within the library setting.

Two major drawbacks to these listings should be noted:

1. The evaluation of products according to one type of criterion (here, in most cases, according to accuracy of sound reproduction) can be misleading. For example, it would be unwise to purchase a receiver on the basis of its FM radio quality score when one intended to use it primarily for playing records.

2. Audio manufacturers are continually updating their existing products as well as introducing new lines. Therefore, ratings such as those provided in this section can rapidly become dated.

These problems can be minimized by determining precisely what the primary purpose of a given rating system appears to be. One can also take solace in the fact that the qualitative ratings of audio equipment tend to be stable in a long-term sense. In other words, what was considered to be good equipment last year is probably good equipment this year, and will probably be of comparable quality the following year.

Medium-Priced Loudspeakers as Rated by *Consumer Reports* in Order of Ability to Reproduce Sound Accurately [1]

Brand name	Accuracy	Power required per speaker
1. Avid 102 (Avid Corp., $130)	91%	13 watts
2. EPI 100 (Epicure Products, $100)	90	15
3. B.I.C. Venturi Formula 2 (B.I.C. Venturi, $120)	88	7
4. Marantz Imperial 5G (Marantz Co., $100)	87	13
5. Lafayette Criterion 2001 (Lafayette Radio, $100)	85	4
6. Micro-Acoustics FRM2 (Micro-Acoustics Corp., $129)	85	8
7. Realistic Optimus 5B (Radio Shack, $115)	84	18
8. Dynaco A35 (Dynaco, $130)	84	11
9. Tempest Lab Series 3 (ESS, $131)	84	7
10. Janszen Z210A (Electronic Industries, $120)	83	35

[1]*Consumer Reports: The 1977 Buying Guide Issue* (Mount Vernon, New York: Consumers Union of the United States, Inc., 1976), pp. 206-207. Other features evaluated include bass response and freedom from bass distortion.

Expensive Loudspeakers as Rated by *Consumer Reports* in Order
of Ability to Reproduce Sound Accurately [1]

Brand name	Accuracy	Power required per speaker
1. Fairfax FX400 (Fairfax Industries, $250)	90%	8 watts
2. Janszen Z412HP (Electronic Industries, $300)	90	17
3. ESS Heil AMT1 (ESS, $299)	89	7
4. E-V Interface: A (Electro Voice, $400/pr. w/equalizer, a specialized add-on tone control.)	88	9 (up to 36 watts with equalizer)
5. JBL Century L100 (James B. Lansing Sound, $273)	88	4
6. Altec Concept EQ 5 (Altec Corp., $475/pr. w/equalizer, a specialized add-on tone control.)	86	6 (up to 30 watts with equalizer)
7. Onkyo 25 (Mitsubi International Corp., $250)	85	5
8. Rectilinear III Lowboy (Rectilinear Research Corp., $299)	85	8
9. Tannoy Mallorcan (Tannoy America, Ltd., $255)	84	6
10. AR 3a (Acoustic Research, $269)	83	15

[1] *Consumer Reports*, pp. 208-209.

Stereo Headphones as Rated by *Consumer Reports* in Order
of Ability to Reproduce Sound Accurately [1]

Brand name	Accuracy	Type
1. Koss Phase/2 (Koss Corp., $75)	84%	Around the ear
2. Superex PEP 77E (Superex Electronics Corp., $125)	82	On the ear
3. Koss ESP 6A (Koss Corp., $130)	82	Around the ear
4. Lafayette F700 (Lafayette Radio Electronics Corp., $35)	80	On the ear
5. Realistic LV10 (Radio Shack, $40)	80	On the ear
6. Pioneer SE 700 (U.S. Pioneer Electronics Corp., $80)	79	On the ear
7. Sennheiser HD 424 (Sennheiser Electronic Corp., $80)	79	On the ear
8. Sennheiser HD 414 (Sennheiser Electronic Corp., $50)	77	On the ear
9. Marantz SE 1S (Marantz Co., $130)	75	Around the ear
10. AKG K180 (North American Phillips Corp., $70)	74	Around the ear

[1]*Consumer Reports,* pp. 210-212.

Low-Priced Receivers as Rated by *Consumer Reports* in Order
of Estimated Overall Quality Based on FM Scores[1] and,
in Case of Ties, by Phonograph [2]

Brand name	FM score	Phonograph score
1. Rotel RX 402 (Rotel of America, $280)	76	99
2. Harman Kardon 330B (Harman/Kardon, $200)	76	93
3. Scott R31S (H.H. Scott, $200)	75	93
4. Pioneer SX 434 (U.S. Pioneer Electronics Corp., $250)	73	95
5. Sansui 551 (Sansui Electronics Corp., $260)	73	94
6. Lafayette LR 1100 (Lafayette Radio Electronics, $250)	72	93
7. Sherwood S7110 (Sherwood Electronics, $250)	71	93
8. Technics SA 5150 (Technics by Panasonic, $230)	70	94
9. JVC VR 5515X (JVC America, $270)	69	96
10. KLH M55A (KLH, $260)	69	85

[1]FM scores take into account frequency response, AM rejection, capture ratio, etc.

[2]*Consumer Reports*, pp. 213-214, 217.

Record Changers as Rated by *Consumer Reports* in Order by
Overall Ratings Score [1]

Brand name	Overall Ratings Score
1. B.I.C. 980 (British Industries Co., $200)	91
2. B.I.C. 960 (British Industries Co., $160)	86
3. Dual 1228 (United Audio Prod., $200)	85
4. Elac/Miracord 760 (Benjamin Electronic Sound Co., $200)	85
5. Realistic/Miracord 46 (Radio Shack, $199)	84
6. Elac/Miracord 820 (Benjamin Electronic Sound Co., $130)	78
7. PE 3044 (Impro Industries, $120)	75
8. BSR McDonald 710 QX (BSR Ltd. of the U.S.A., $250)	74
9. BSR McDonald 810 QX (BSR Ltd. of the U.S.A., $300)	74
10. Dual 1225 (United Audio Prod., $140)	71

[1] *Consumer Reports*, pp. 222-223. The overall ratings score
takes into account freedom from flutter and rumble, speed
accuracy, vertical tracking force, effective tone-arm mass,
etc.

Low-Priced Compact Stereo Systems as Rated by *Consumer
Reports* in Order of Estimated Overall Quality [1]

Brand name

---

1. Zenith F584W
   (Zenith Radio Corp., $210)

2. Sylvania CS4720
   (GTE Sylvania, $200)

3. Sony HP 161
   (Sony Corp. of America, $200)

4. J.C. Penny Cat. No. 3291
   (J.C. Penny, $195 plus shipping)

5. Sanyo GXT 4310
   (Sanyo Electric, $180)

6. Panasonic RE 7014
   (Panasonic Co., $180)

7. Capehart 8TP72
   (Capehart Corp., $200)

8. General Electric SC 3213
   (General Electric, $190)

9. Juliette C43282
   (Topp Electronics, $200)

10. Soundesign 4769623
    (Soundesign Corp., $185)

11. Wards Cat. No. 6432
    (Montgomery Ward, $188 plus shipping)

All of the above systems have the following features: 33-1/3-,
45-, and 78-rpm turntable speeds; FM/AM stereo tuner; FM stereo
indicator light; function selector switch; headphone jack; one
pair of auxiliary inputs; line cord indoor FM antenna and
terminals for outdoor FM antenna. All except the Sony have
an automatic 45-rpm adapter, and all except the Sylvania and
Panasonic models (which are hinged) have a nonhinged dust cover.
Most have separate tone controls for bass and treble, automatic
last-record power shutoff, cuing lever, and six-record changer
capacity.

---

[1] *Consumer Reports*, p. 228.

Stereo Phono Cartridges as Rated by *Consumer Reports* by
Groups in Order of Estimated Overall Quality [1]

Primary Group	Shure V15 Type III
Secondary Group	ADC XLM, Elac STS 444E, Ortofon M15E, Philips GP 412, Pickering XV15/400E, Pickering XV15/750E, Shure M91ED, Stanton 681EE
Third Group	ADC Q36, ADC 26, ADC 220XE, Audio-Technica AT11E, B&O SP12, Empire 66E/X, Empire 999SE/X, Empire 10000ZE/X, Pickering V15 Micro IV ATE, Pickering XV15/1200E, Shure M44E, Shure M75EJ Type 11, Stanton 500E, Stanton 600E.
Fourth Group	Decca London MK5, Ering XV15/140E

[1]*Consumer Reports*, pp. 225-226.